Prepared by the Special Publications Division
National Geographic Society, Washington, D. C.

Nature's World of
WONDERS

NATURE'S WORLD OF WONDERS

Contributing Authors: RON FISHER, WILLIAM R. GRAY,
  LOREN McINTYRE, THOMAS O'NEILL,
  CYNTHIA RUSS RAMSAY

Contributing Photographers: DAVID AUSTEN,
  PAUL CHESLEY, GEORG GERSTER, LOREN McINTYRE,
  GEORGE F. MOBLEY

Published by
The National Geographic Society
GILBERT M. GROSVENOR, *President*
MELVIN M. PAYNE, *Chairman of the Board*
OWEN R. ANDERSON, *Executive Vice President*
ROBERT L. BREEDEN, *Vice President, Publications and
  Educational Media*

Prepared by
The Special Publications Division
DONALD J. CRUMP, *Editor*
PHILIP B. SILCOTT, *Associate Editor*
WILLIAM L. ALLEN, WILLIAM R. GRAY, *Senior Editors*

Staff for this book
MARGERY G. DUNN, *Managing Editor*
DENNIS R. DIMICK, *Picture Editor*
MARIANNE R. KOSZORUS, *Art Director*
KAREN M. KOSTYAL, *Project Coordinator*
MARILYN WILBUR CLEMENT, STEPHEN J. HUBBARD,
  KAREN M. KOSTYAL, *Researchers;* CATHERINE HERBERT
  HOWELL, ALICE K. JABLONSKY, *Assistant Researchers;*
  CAROLE L. TYLER, *Research Assistant*
JANE H. BUXTON, MARILYN WILBUR CLEMENT, LOUIS DE
  LA HABA, TONI EUGENE, KATHLEEN M. GIBBONS,
  KAREN M. KOSTYAL, JENNIFER C. URQUHART,
  SUZANNE VENINO, *Picture Legend Writers*
JODY BOLT, *Map Artist and Consulting Art Director*
JOHN D. GARST, JR., SUSAN M. JOHNSTON, JUDITH BELL
  SIEGEL, ANDREW J. SWITHINBANK, *Map Research and
  Production*
CAROL A. ROCHELEAU, *Illustrations Assistant*

Engraving, Printing, and Product Manufacture
ROBERT W. MESSER, *Manager*
GEORGE V. WHITE, *Production Manager*
GREGORY STORER, *Production Project Manager*
MARK R. DUNLEVY, RICHARD A. McCLURE, DAVID V.
  SHOWERS, *Assistant Production Managers;* KATHERINE H.
  DONOHUE, *Senior Production Assistant;* MARY A.
  BENNETT, *Production Assistant;* JULIA F. WARNER,
  Production Staff Assistant
NANCY F. BERRY, C. REBECCA BITTLE, PAMELA A. BLACK,
  NETTIE BURKE, MARY ELIZABETH DAVIS, CLAIRE M.
  DOIG, JANET A. DUSTIN, ROSAMUND GARNER, VICTORIA
  D. GARRETT, JANE R. HALPIN, NANCY J. HARVEY,
  JOAN HURST, ARTEMIS S. LAMPATHAKIS, KATHERINE R.
  LEITCH, VIRGINIA W. McCOY, MARY EVELYN
  McKINNEY, CLEO E. PETROFF, VICTORIA I. PISCOPO,
  TAMMY PRESLEY, SHERYL A. PROHOVICH, KATHLEEN T.
  SHEA, KATHERYN M. SLOCUM, *Staff Assistants*
DIANNE L. HOSMER, *Indexer*

*Ayers Rock, in the Australian outback, tempts
visitors to clamber to its summit. Pages 2-3: A
causeway splits cloud reflections on Lake Magadi in
Kenya. Page 1: Torrents thunder into the Devil's
Throat of South America's Iguazú Falls.*

PAUL CHESLEY

Contents

In Iceland, snow streaks a glaciated landscape, and
clouds blanket the slopes of an active volcano. The
island regularly witnesses violent phenomena—erupting
volcanoes, spouting geysers, steaming vents. Glaciers
cover more than 10 percent of the ''land of ice and fire.''

Foreword

THE ICY VASTNESS of Antarctica, the towering peaks of the Himalayas, the shifting sands of the Sahara: How these wondrous works of nature beckoned from the pages of NATIONAL GEOGRAPHIC when I was a boy growing up in Cincinnati, Ohio. Each month, when my family's copy arrived, I sought out articles that took me to far-flung reaches and expanded my vision of nature's wonders. As they did in many young people, those stories kindled myriad dreams—of following in the footsteps of polar explorer Richard Byrd, of scaling Mount Everest, of reaching the elusive sources of the Nile. And, over the years, some of those boyhood dreams have become reality. Others remain dreams.

In this welcome book, five seasoned travelers lead us on journeys to all seven continents in search of but a few of nature's wonders. Collectively, the chapters go beyond mere description of nature's creations and explanation of the processes that produce them. Indeed, the book brings the realization that nature is complex and simple, powerful and delicate, fleeting and enduring. For me, these perceptive accounts and supporting photographs call forth vivid memories and kindle new dreams.

As I ventured south to the Antarctic with Cynthia Ramsay, I remembered how amazed I was years ago when, as a member of Admiral Byrd's staff, I sailed through Neptune's Bellows—a narrow break in the rim of Deception Island—into the submerged caldera that forms one of the world's perfect natural harbors. Reading Ron Fisher's chapter on Europe, I recalled the contentment of basking in sunny solitude on the summit of the Matterhorn one July noon and pondering the endless etching of the cirque glaciers that had helped create my perch in space.

Following Ron to Asia, I harked back to a blustery October day on top of Mount Fuji. Around the conical base, larches gave off a deep golden glimmer as mauve and gray cumulus clouds welled up from the south. Precursors of a typhoon, they signaled it was time to descend.

Then, in the Himalayas, I felt once again the euphoria of a day in 1963 when I stood on the summit of Everest with fellow climber Lute Jerstad. Wind-whipped, cold, and spent, we surveyed the purple-brown expanse of the Tibetan Plateau. My oxygen-starved mind jumped from thought to thought. Two were: "A few feet beneath this snow is fossil-bearing limestone 350 million years old that has been thrust up more than 6 miles by the tectonic crunch of continental plates" and "How small and insignificant we are in the realm of nature."

Some of the wonders visited in this book are accessible to many of us. Others are in remote fastnesses that few of us will ever explore firsthand. But we all can indulge our wanderlust and curiosity vicariously. I hope that you derive as much joy from the journeys that follow as I have.

Sunlight, clouds, and swirling snow move over craggy facets of the world's crowning jewels—the Himalayas. This loftiest of all mountain ranges, whose Sanskrit name means "abode of snow," contains dozens of peaks higher than 25,000 feet and annually draws scores of climbing expeditions.

NICHOLAS DEVORE III

Barry C. Bishop, Ph.D.
Committee for Research and Exploration
National Geographic Society

Africa

By William R. Gray
Photographs by
George F. Mobley

J ust as it cleared the horizon, the dawning sun fired the billowing spray of Victoria Falls, creating an evanescent veil of rose and gold that faded as quickly as it had formed. A moment later, sunlight touched the falls. I stood there, awestruck.

The Zambezi River, coursing eastward between Zambia and Zimbabwe, broadens and slows as it nears Victoria Falls. Suddenly plunging over a ledge of lava, the river produces a staggering spectacle— a curtain of water more than a mile wide. Victoria Falls is so immense that it cannot be encompassed in one glance. To appreciate it fully, I needed not only my sight but all my other senses as well. Indeed, the local name for the falls derives from its auditory impact: *Mosi-oa-tunya*, the Kololo people named it, "smoke that thunders."

The continent of Africa and the geologically related areas of the Middle East present an amazing diversity of attractions. Even their names evoke a sense of mystery and excitement: Zambezi . . . Kilimanjaro . . . Ngorongoro . . . Aqaba. For two months I would seek out Africa's wonders and visit some of the most majestic natural features on earth: the Sahara—the largest hot desert; the Nile—the longest river; the Rift Valley system—a geologic marvel that rends the earth from Malawi in southeastern Africa north almost to Turkey. I would also learn about the lore and the history of the land—and about the European explorers who first ventured into Africa, explorers such as Richard Francis Burton, Henry Morton Stanley, and the incomparable Livingstone.

Born in Scotland, David Livingstone first voyaged to Africa in 1840 as a missionary-doctor. For more than 30 years he healed the sick, proclaimed the novel message of Christianity, and explored more of the continent than any European before him. Victoria Falls was just one of his many discoveries. "It had never been seen before by European eyes," he wrote in November 1855, "but scenes so lovely must have been gazed upon by angels in their flight."

Tumbling over the ledge, the Zambezi cascades into a gorge 350 feet below. The gorge, more than 200 feet across, parallels the falls and is broken only in one place—where the river has cut through the rock to continue on its course. Livingstone conjectured that the gorge was created by a cataclysmic cracking of the earth. Scientists today link the existence of Victoria Falls not to an isolated event, but to the geologic development of Africa and to the global system of plate tectonics.

The theory of plate tectonics proposes that the crust of the continents and of the ocean floor is broken into many large slabs—called plates—that move slowly over the much hotter and more plastic rock below. When plates collide, energy is released in the form of earthquakes and volcanic eruptions, and great mountain ranges may be thrust up. Where plates split apart, deep rifts and ridges form, accompanied by earthquakes and volcanic activity.

Suffused with dawn's light, clouds of spray boil up from Victoria Falls, the "smoke that thunders." Here in western Zimbabwe, the Zambezi River plummets 350 feet over a mile-wide basaltic ledge to create an immense curtain of falling water. Scottish missionary David Livingstone, who explored the continent for some 30 years beginning in 1841, pronounced the falls "the most wonderful sight I had witnessed in Africa."

N.G.S. PHOTOGRAPHER JAMES L. STANFIELD

(Continued on page 16)

*L*ow-lying clouds trace the contours of Kenya's Great Rift Valley,
    a spectacular segment in a 5,000-mile-long system of cracks in the
    earth's crust extending from southeastern Africa almost to Turkey.
Subterranean stresses split the land, creating a rift between parallel fault
lines. Giraffes (right) roam the seasonally dusty savannas.

Following pages: Flamingos flock to the alkaline waters of Lake Bogoria in
Kenya; a youth bathes beside a steaming geyser. Hot springs laden with salt
and other minerals feed several such soda lakes in the rift.

"The northeastern part of Africa appears to be an ocean in the making," geologist Kathleen Crane told me. A staff scientist at the Lamont-Doherty Geological Observatory of Columbia University in New York, Kathy has studied the rifting boundaries between tectonic plates in the Pacific, Atlantic, and Arctic Oceans and in Africa. "A plate boundary is forming along most of the length of Africa. It's like a zipper slowly being opened. Isolated rifting and spreading—with associated volcanic and seismic activity—has occurred for millions of years throughout much of East Africa. Now it looks as if the smaller isolated rift zones may all be joining into one large rift. The zipper is opening in the north, in Djibouti and Ethiopia, and may continue to unzip all the way through Kenya, Tanzania, Malawi, and perhaps farther south."

Young and energetic, Kathy has a gift for simplifying complex geologic theories. "About a hundred million years ago," she explained, "enormous molten disturbances within the earth uplifted part of Africa's crust, producing broad domes. Three of these domes are in Ethiopia, Kenya, and the Zambia-Zimbabwe region. Large stresses built up around the domes, and the earth ruptured into radiating cracks and fissures. About 23 million years ago, some of the cracks started spreading, and the system of African rifts that we know today began."

I asked Kathy what she foresaw. "Well, if the rifting continues—if the zipper is entirely open—the eastern section of Africa will become a mini-continent drifting on its own plate." She paused for a moment. "To me, the earth is like a motion picture. It's dynamic, and everything is moving through time. But it's frustrating that most of the processes are so slow. It may be 50 million years before we know what the end result in Africa is, and I don't think I'll be around then."

Before I left Victoria Falls, I related it to what Kathy had told me of Africa's geologic past. After the doming began in this region, floods of lava were released on the surface of the earth at thicknesses of hundreds of feet. Millions of years later, the Zambezi River began to follow fissures in the lava, eroding it and carving a series of waterfalls. A great fissure at a right angle to the river marks the site of Victoria Falls.

From the falls, I paralleled the course of the Zambezi to the small nation of Malawi. Lake Malawi—formerly known as Nyasa and called the "lake of stars"—occupies about one-fourth of the country and fills that portion of the Rift Valley system. South of Lake Malawi the rift widens into an undulating valley marked by lush mountains and steep escarpments. The Zomba Plateau, a huge hump of forested rock riven by sparkling streams, soars several thousand feet above the rift floor. The plateau offers panoramic views of the rift, but only when the weather is clear. I waited for several days; all I saw was the inside of clouds.

I had the view described to me by someone who should know—Lt. Col. Brian Burgess, whose home perches on the very edge of the plateau. We sat on his veranda sipping strong black Malawi coffee.

"It's idyllic," said Brian, a retired colonial police officer who came to Malawi—then called Nyasaland—28 years ago from England and asked never to be transferred. "The land is rolling and green; flowers grow everywhere. The earth is fertile, and the climate is perfect. I sit here for hours at a time and simply drink in the beauty."

The mist eddied and thinned for a moment as Brian spoke, but all I could see was a vague emerald blur far below. I had to be content with

"some of the most majestic natural features on earth"

Brian's description and with the riot of color in his garden—scarlet hibiscus, mauve bougainvillea, and roses of a dozen subtle hues.

Brighter skies awaited me in Tanzania, where I began to explore the eastern arm of the Rift Valley system. North of Malawi, the rift splits into two dramatic sections. One cuts through central Tanzania and Kenya into Ethiopia and Djibouti; the other curls northwestward along Zaire's border with Tanzania, Burundi, Rwanda, and Uganda.

In northern Tanzania I found two stupendous natural wonders that attest the volcanic activity of the rift. Kilimanjaro soars regally above the rolling grasslands of East Africa, drawing the eye to its glaciered summit from a hundred miles in any direction. Its appearance changes with the time of day and the vagaries of sunlight. One dawn it was bathed in delicate shades of pink; puffy clouds draped its shoulders like a mantle of

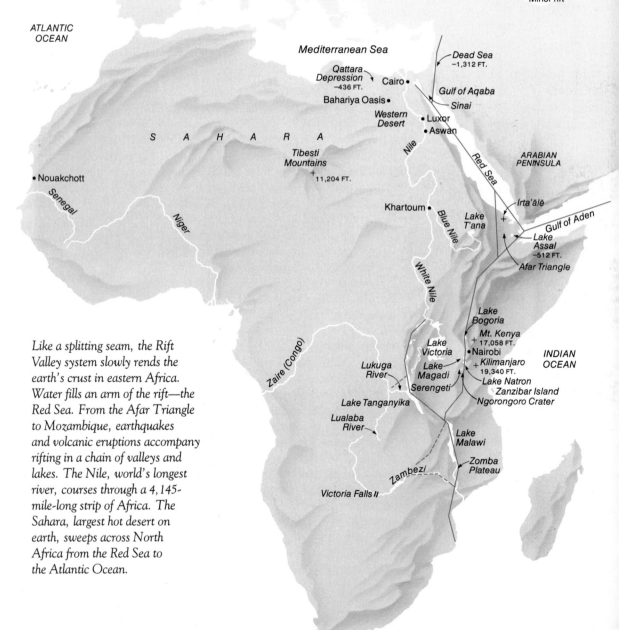

Rift Valley System
—— Major rift
----- Minor rift

Like a splitting seam, the Rift Valley system slowly rends the earth's crust in eastern Africa. Water fills an arm of the rift—the Red Sea. From the Afar Triangle to Mozambique, earthquakes and volcanic eruptions accompany rifting in a chain of valleys and lakes. The Nile, world's longest river, courses through a 4,145-mile-long strip of Africa. The Sahara, largest hot desert on earth, sweeps across North Africa from the Red Sea to the Atlantic Ocean.

ermine on a king. Later, during a rain-drenched evening, Kilimanjaro was a blue-gray monolith, surly and unforgiving.

Johann Rebmann, a German missionary, was the first European to see the 19,340-foot bulk of Kilimanjaro, the highest mountain on the continent. On May 11, 1848, he noted, "I fancied I saw the summit . . . covered with a dazzlingly white cloud. My guide called the white which I saw merely 'Beredi,' cold; it was perfectly clear to me, however, that it could be nothing else but snow."

When Rebmann reported his discovery to the august Royal Geographical Society of London, he was ridiculed. Snow in central Africa? Practically on the Equator? Preposterous. One member reportedly dismissed Rebmann's observations as "figments of imagination . . . of reasonable evidence of perpetual snow there is not a tittle offered." Only years later, when other European explorers had penetrated the region and observed the perpetual snows of Kilimanjaro and Africa's second highest peak, 17,058-foot Mount Kenya, was Rebmann vindicated.

The other volcanic marvel in Tanzania that I explored was Ngorongoro Crater. A huge caldera, Ngorongoro spreads some 10 miles by 12, and the floor drops 2,000 feet below the rim. Once a towering mountain, Ngorongoro collapsed inward after the molten material underlying it had been spewed out, leaving a vast empty chamber and a weakened foundation that could not support the weight of the rock above.

Standing on the rim at sunset, I surveyed Ngorongoro. My guide told me the name means "huge hole." Rather prosaic, I thought, but it did capture the essence of the place. Grass the color of a lion's back blankets the floor of the crater, broken here and there by stands of trees. The only bright color I noticed was what appeared to be a pink film on the surface of a shallow lake. Early next morning, I descended into the crater by Land-Rover and discovered that the pink film was actually thousands of flamingos; they were feeding on algae in the lake.

I spent the rest of the day exploring Ngorongoro and discovering its marvelous wildlife. If I saw thousands of flamingos, I also saw thousands of wildebeests, hundreds of zebras, scores of gazelles, dozens of baboons, and several kinds of predators—lions, cheetahs, jackals, hyenas. The crater lies at the center of the 3,200-square-mile Ngorongoro Conservation Area. During the dry season, great herds of wildebeests, zebras, and antelopes come here for an assured source of water.

The most startling animal encounter I had that day occurred at the top of a steep knoll. Clearing the rise in my Land-Rover, I came almost face to face with two burly lions. At first they regarded me coolly; then they ignored me. They rested on their haunches, at times watching a distant herd of wildebeests, at times dozing or perhaps daydreaming. One lion got up, stretched, flicked his tail, and approached the other. He leaned down and rubbed his face in the other's mane. There was no immediate response. Then, without warning, the resting lion cuffed the other with a paw and roared—a powerful, primal sound. The first lion stepped back, stared for a moment, then settled back down. I left them placidly surveying their domain.

The early explorers of the rift region of Tanzania and Kenya worried less about wild animals than they did about the tall, formidable Masai tribespeople. Today the Masai in both countries still live a free life, herding cattle as they have for hundreds of years.

"The Masai occupy a region in southern Kenya and northern Tanzania that includes the rift," Igor Loupekine told me, "and they live in *manyattas*, traditional village communities." Igor, born of White Russian parents in Egypt, founded the geology department of the University of Nairobi 27 years ago. Over the years he has become the leading local expert on the Great Rift Valley in Kenya. A zestful man with a beard, Igor agreed to guide me into the rift.

Early one lustrous January morning, we jounced out of Nairobi in Igor's Volkswagen bus, heading southwest.

"Ah, you'll love the rift," Igor said, smiling as he warmed to his favorite subject. "Geologically, it is one of the most complex and fascinating regions on earth. And it's beautiful, too. It's the longest single continuous rift on land, and that's impressive. What we have here is the first stage of the rifting process; the land is fractured and faulted and slowly pulling apart. When the rift areas of Kenya reach the next stage, it will be like the Red Sea—underwater. Once the African and Arabian coasts of the Red Sea were together, but rifting split them apart. Finally, the sea filled the rift. I think that will probably happen here eventually."

After driving over a dry, rumpled landscape for an hour, we reached the Great Rift Valley. Igor parked the bus, and we walked to the edge of a steep escarpment that dropped away dramatically for several hundred feet. A flat plain at the bottom stretched a short distance before it too dropped sharply off.

"As you can see," Igor said with a sweep of his arm, "the rift is not a simple, single break in the earth. It is made up of many faults, which are like stairsteps. And the land in front of us has been faulted repeatedly."

He showed me the geologic chart for this section of the rift; it was a tangle of black lines, most of them oriented north-south. "Every one of these black lines indicates a fault running along the Rift Valley," he explained. "And there are hundreds of faults, some of them major, but most of them minor."

We returned to the bus and descended to the rift floor. Every few feet, it seemed, the road would take us up or down a small rise. "Each of those humps," Igor said, "is the result of a fault. The earth has been split and offset. What you see here is geology in action." The rifting and faulting process has produced a tortured landscape. Earth and rock in shades ranging from magenta to black were exposed everywhere, as if wrenched from the ground.

We continued through the rift to Lake Magadi, near the Kenya-Tanzania border. Magadi is one of the famous soda lakes of the Great Rift Valley, lakes that are composed not of fresh water but mostly of mineral-rich liquids bubbling from hot springs. "Lake" is misleading, because Magadi is largely dry; it consists of small, scattered pools, except during the rainy season when runoff floods the lake bed. Despite its lack of water, Magadi sparkled in the scorching sun. "Evaporite," Igor explained. "The material left by evaporation. Here it's chiefly composed of the mineral trona—sodium sesquicarbonate."

I crunched across the lake and picked up a chunk of evaporite, which is mined and processed for soda ash. It was crumbly and delicate, and the minerals had formed in lacy patterns that reflected the sunlight in diamondlike bursts.

Glancing up at the craggy escarpments around me, I realized that I was standing at the bottom of the Great Rift Valley—the very basement of Africa. In some places that basement *(Continued on page 26)*

"Kilimanjaro was a blue-gray monolith, surly and unforgiving"

19

*C*rown of the continent, Kilimanjaro juts 19,340 feet above the grasslands of Tanzania and Kenya. Kibo Peak, most recent of three eruption sites in the dormant volcano, bears three concentric craters, the largest measuring one and a half miles across (above). Perpetual glaciers drape the summit, only about 200 miles south of the Equator. Beyond Kibo looms the jagged formation called Mawenzi, remnant of an ancient eruption. "As wide as all the world, great, high, and unbelievably white in the sun," wrote Ernest Hemingway of the volcano in "The Snows of Kilimanjaro." At the base of the majestic mountain, wildebeests forage in Kenya's Amboseli Game Reserve (opposite).

*S*mall wonder: On spindly legs, a young zebra totters near its mother in Ngorongoro Conservation Area,
a 3,200-square-mile reserve in Tanzania. At its center lies Ngorongoro Crater, a huge caldera whose
floor covers 102 square miles. Africa's living treasure—its diverse wildlife—finds protection in numerous
refuges. Northwest of Ngorongoro, a cheetah and her two cubs (above) rest on a sunny savanna in Serengeti
National Park. Established more than 60 years ago, the park now shelters one of the greatest concentrations
of large mammals on earth. Thousands of zebras and wildebeests graze the Serengeti Plain (below).

Overleaf: Wine-red waters of Lake Natron in Tanzania, stained by a seasonal bloom of algae, spread beneath
a low-flying Cessna; a crust of soda turns pink as it dries. Mineral-rich springs nourish Natron, more than 500
square miles of shallows and white soda flats overlying black mud. Many of East Africa's four million flamingos
nest at the lake, feeding on the abundant algae that tolerate the high alkalinity.

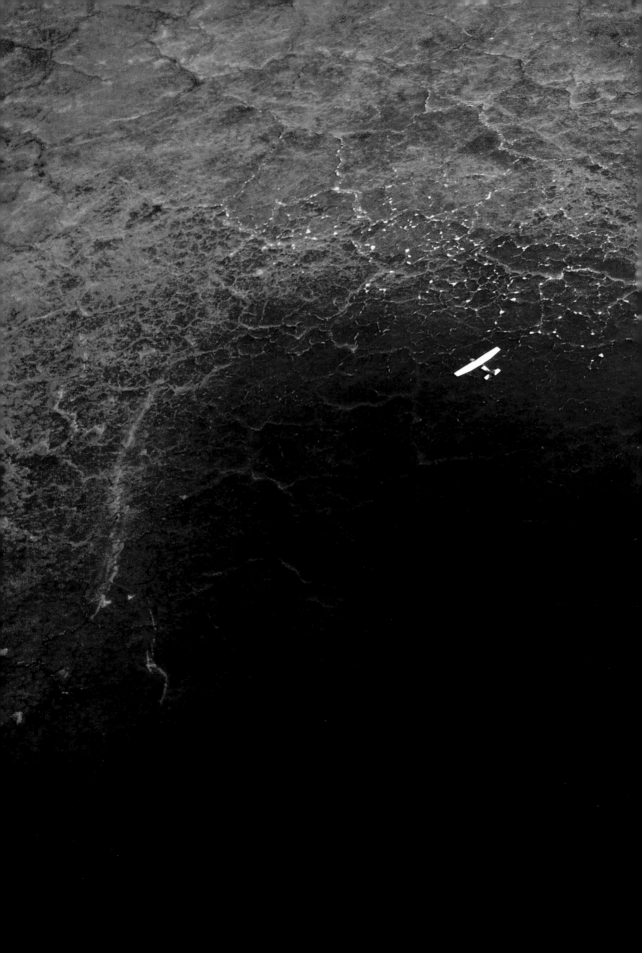

drops deeper than in others. In fact, the lowest points in both Africa and Asia are parts of the rift system—Lake Assal in Djibouti at 512 feet below sea level and the Dead Sea on the border between Israel and Jordan at minus 1,312 feet.

"Djibouti is in one of the most tectonically active parts of the rift system," Kathy Crane had explained to me. "It lies near the juncture of three rift arms—the one underlying the Red Sea, the one underlying the Gulf of Aden, and the Rift Valley system in Africa. The geologic stresses are tremendous, and the frequency of earthquakes and volcanic eruptions is staggering. What happens here may determine whether or not the African rift will continue to grow. If it does, then East Africa may slowly split off from the rest of the continent."

Bouncing by four-wheel-drive vehicle far into the backcountry of Djibouti, I could see what Kathy meant. It is a raw volcanic wilderness. The track that my guide, Hamadou, and I followed led across miles of lava flows, past dozens of cinder cones, along fault scarps that looked as fresh as the loaf of French bread we had bought in the capital for lunch. And fresh the activity is. As we drove, Hamadou kept up a litany of information: "This lava is from the eruption of 1978. . . . We're driving here on a new track—the old one was destroyed by an earthquake. . . . That little volcano is from the eruption of 1974. . . . None of this lava was here when I made my first trip ten years ago." And on and on.

Fists full of rice seedlings, a boy shadowboxes at an irrigation project near Lake Victoria. The Ahero Rice Pilot Scheme—an attempt to improve Kenya's agricultural production— diverts the waters of the Nyando River to irrigate rice fields. Planting (below) continues past sunset. The Nyando flows into Victoria, Africa's largest lake and main feeder of the White Nile.

After hours of slow, bone-jarring progress through this desolate countryside, we began to descend. A dense haze hung over the land, and through it I could just detect a gray smudge bordered by a fringe of white. "Lake Assal?" I asked. Hamadou nodded. But it took two more hours of head-bumping, spine-shaking driving to reach the lake, which is fed in part by the bitter waters of hot springs. The color of Lake Assal is haunting—a sort of peacock blue that has become faded by too many years in the sun. The color is intensified by the platinum hue of the surrounding hills and by the glittering white of the salt deposited on the shoreline.

Steam wafts from a lake of molten lava in the crater of Ethiopia's Irta'ālē, one of several volcanoes in the Afar Triangle, lowest and most geologically active part of Africa. Afar tribesmen of this region call Irta'ālē "smoking mountain." It last erupted in the 1960s. About a dozen active volcanoes in the rift system attest the earth-splitting forces at work on the continent.

Stretching my stiff muscles, I wandered along the shore of the lake as Hamadou slept. I felt certain that this was one of the most isolated places I had ever visited. And so I was startled to see a caravan of three men and a dozen camels coming toward me. Their dress and their noble handsomeness told me they were members of the Afar tribe. Another clue to their identity was the long, curving Afar knife—the size of a machete—that hung in a cowhide sheath from each man's waist.

As the men approached, I smiled, nodded, and raised my hand. They scrutinized me for a moment, and then their faces warmed with broad smiles. They quickly went to work prying large chunks of salt from the lakeshore and placing them in sacks strapped to their camels. For centuries people have taken salt from this forbidding region and traded it across much of northeastern Africa. At times it has been worth more than its weight in gold. Watching the Afar tribesmen, I felt that I had been transported back in time.

Standing beside the gently lapping waters of the Dead Sea in Israel, I knew I had returned to the 20th century. A cluster of resort hotels jutted skyward to my right, and a blacktop highway behind me carried busload after busload of visitors on package tours of the Holy Land. The contrast with the remote desolation of Lake Assal was startling.

Forty-five miles long and nine wide, the Dead Sea fills a section of a huge shear zone in the rift system. Angling up the narrow Gulf of Aqaba from the Red Sea, the system borders highlands where the Sinai meets the Arabian Peninsula, then opens into the fault that holds the Dead Sea, the lowest place on land. North of the Dead Sea, the fault slices up the valley of the Jordan River, past the Sea of Galilee, and into Lebanon. It finally ends near the Turkish border.

I had journeyed over 5,000 miles of this ever-changing system, from the dancing spray of Victoria Falls to the torpid waters of the Dead

Sea. Between these two extremes, high in forested mountains above the rift, rises one of the world's great rivers. It begins as a tiny spring, gains size and strength as it flows through sprawling lakes and over cataracts, then slows to a stately pace as it winds across some 2,000 miles of sun-baked desert on its way to the Mediterranean Sea.

Through the ages, the mighty Nile, at 4,145 miles the longest river on earth, has been a source of life—and of mystery. Without it, the great civilization of Egypt might never have arisen; today most of Egypt's 45 million people live along its fertile banks. For centuries the Nile has enticed explorers and adventurers. Many sought the wealth they imagined lay at its farthest reaches; others simply wanted to solve the geographic puzzle of its sources.

In 1768 a Scottish aristocrat named James Bruce set out to discover the ultimate source of the Nile. For two years Bruce confronted hardship and war as he struggled from the Red Sea across what today is Ethiopia.

In central Ethiopia, Bruce followed the Ābay River from Lake T'ana to its headwaters—a small marsh in the midst of steep, rugged mountains. He rejoiced, certain that he had traced the Nile to its source. He was partially correct: He had reached *a* source. At Khartoum, capital of Sudan, the two major branches of the Nile merge. Bruce had reached the source of the eastern branch, the Blue Nile, which, while supplying most of the water to the main Nile, is more than 1,000 miles shorter than the other branch, the White Nile. It would take many years for the source waters of the White Nile to be discovered.

Rumors persisted of a vast inland sea—Arabs called it the Sea of Ujiji—from which the Nile supposedly issued. To lead an expedition there, the Royal Geographical Society selected Richard Burton, an audacious explorer who had spent many years in outposts of Asia and Africa. His goal always had been to discover what he called the "Coy Fountains"—the source of the Nile. With him was John Hanning

Overleaf: An aerial view of Irta'ālē's lava lake resembles an abstract painting. Ribbons of red-hot magma crack the thin crust on the surface, and lava fountains shoot high into the air. Only a few of the world's volcanoes hold permanent lava lakes; this one measures at least 150 feet across.

29

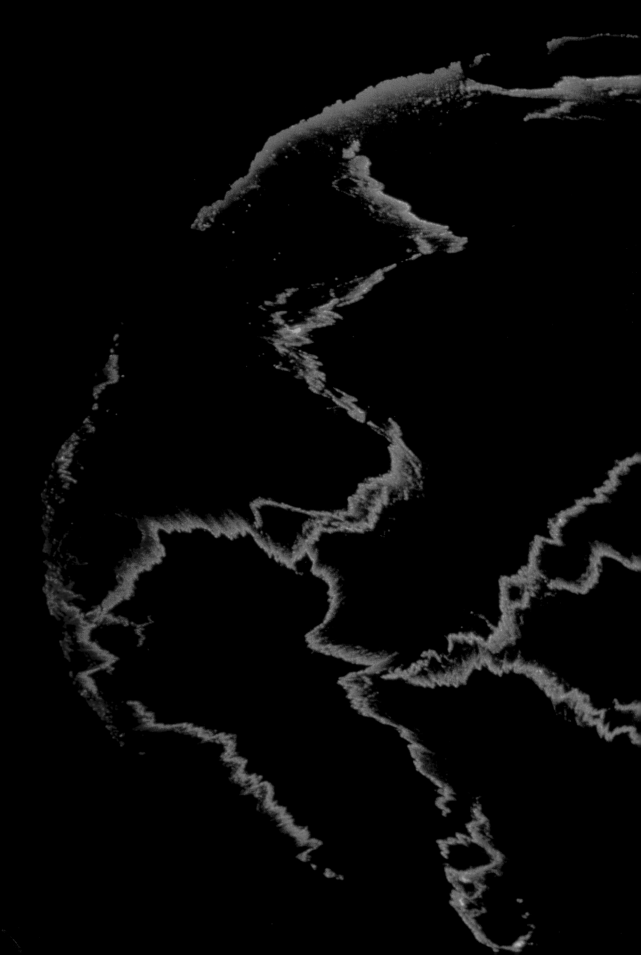

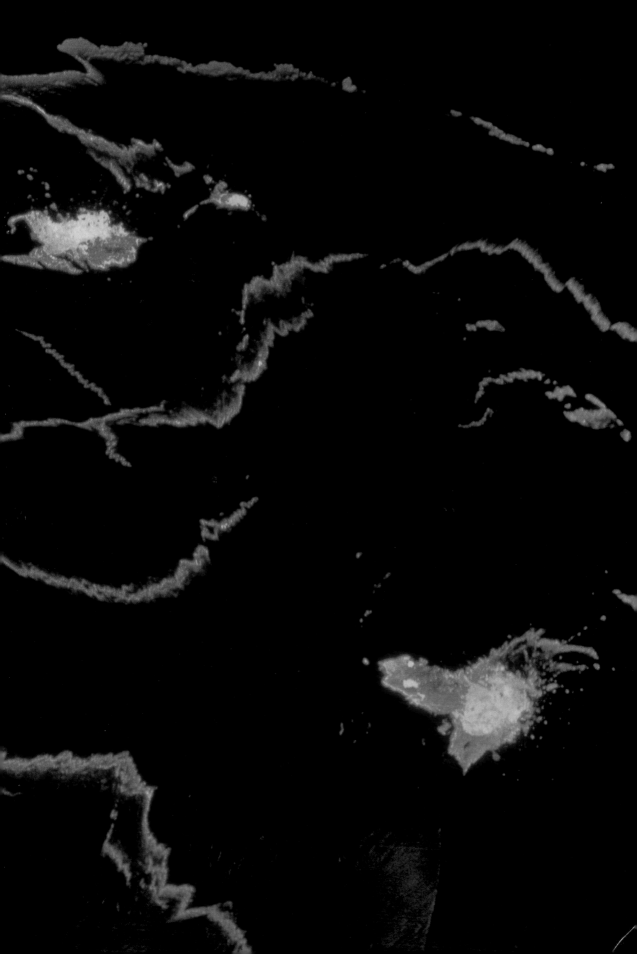

Speke, an army officer who also had left England for more adventurous regions. Unlike Burton, Speke was disciplined and methodical.

In June 1857 Burton and Speke left Zanzibar with a caravan of porters and guards and enough ammunition and trade goods to last for two years. Infection and disease beset the pair as they labored through jungles and swamps and across mountains. On February 13, 1858, they struggled to the top of a hill so steep that Speke's donkey died from the strain of climbing. Half blind, Burton could barely make out a streak of reflected light. It was what they sought—the Sea of Ujiji, now called Lake Tanganyika. They were told by Arab slavers that a river called the Ruzizi flowed north from the lake. Convinced that the river must be the Nile, they reconnoitered in two large canoes manned by 55 paddlers.

"I felt sick at heart," Burton wrote after he discovered that the Ruzizi flowed not north, but south into the Sea of Ujiji.

In the meantime, they had heard rumors of another, even larger lake to the north. Burton chose to stay behind while Speke set out with a small company on a six-week expedition. When he came to the shore of a seemingly limitless expanse of water, he "no longer felt any doubt that the lake at my feet gave birth to that interesting river, the source of which has been the subject of so much speculation, and the object of so many explorers." He named the lake Victoria, for his queen.

Hearing of Speke's discovery, Burton was skeptical. There was no evidence that a river flowed from the lake, and even if one did, there was no evidence that it was the Nile. A deep bitterness developed between Speke and Burton that was to last the rest of their days and to divide the learned community of Europe into two camps: those who believed that

"the bottom of the Great Rift Valley -- the very basement of Africa"

"A landscape of terror, of hardships, of death," an explorer in 1928 described the Danakil Depression in the Afar Triangle, where brightly colored salts lace pools of brine (opposite). Uplifting separated the Danakil from the Red Sea tens of thousands of years ago. Today seawater bubbles from alkaline springs, which deposit salt leached from volcanic rock. At right, miners pry salt slabs from a lake bed.

GEORG GERSTER (ABOVE AND OPPOSITE)

Speke had discovered the source of the Nile in Lake Victoria and those who wanted more proof.

In 1860 Speke led a second expedition to Lake Victoria. It was another agonizing venture, beset by disease and hostile tribesmen. Not until July 28, 1862, did Speke sight an outlet from the lake: a huge river tumbling over a waterfall and heading north. Speke was convinced more than ever that this was the Nile, but he did not circumnavigate the lake or follow the course of the river to prove it. In London doubts about the Nile's source persisted.

The Royal Geographical Society called upon the one man they felt could dispel these doubts—David Livingstone. He accepted, but on his own terms: He would go not only as a geographer, but also as a missionary and a crusader against the slave trade. Leaving Zanzibar in 1866, he spent seven arduous years slogging through the jungles of central Africa. He discovered more lakes and rivers, one of them named the Lualaba, but shed no new light on the Nile question. Racked by fever and starvation, he died in the spring of 1873, at age 59. Eighteen months earlier, however, he had entrusted his quest to another man.

Henry Morton Stanley, a tough and flamboyant journalist, had been sent to Africa by his newspaper, the *New York Herald*, to find Livingstone, from whom little had been heard for five years. Stanley discovered Livingstone on the shore of Lake Tanganyika, and their meeting changed his life. The two men spent five months together, and Stanley was touched by Livingstone's deep faith, his love of Africa and its peoples, his abiding passion for exploration and geography.

In 1874 Stanley embarked on a monumental expedition with three overriding objectives: first, to circumnavigate Lake Victoria and determine if it was one huge lake or a group of smaller ones and to discover if Speke's river was actually the Nile; second, to circumnavigate Lake Tanganyika and decide if its outflow could possibly be a source of the Nile; third, to find Livingstone's Lualaba River and follow it to the sea.

In one incredible 999-day expedition, Stanley succeeded in all three missions. He confirmed that Speke had "discovered the largest inland sea on the continent of Africa . . . as well as its outlet." Stanley was sure it was a source of the Nile. He established that the sluggish outflow of Lake Tanganyika, the Lukuga River, flows west toward the Congo River—now the Zaire—not north toward the Nile. Then, striking west, Stanley came upon the Lualaba in what today is east-central Zaire. Braving cannibals and head-hunters, diseases and starvation, he and his depleted, exhausted entourage followed the Lualaba, which becomes the Congo, all the way to the Atlantic Ocean.

For half a century after Stanley's explorations, the southernmost source stream of the Nile remained undiscovered. An obscure German explorer, Burkhart Waldecker, had searched diligently for that elusive

"the longest river on earth... a source of life-- and of mystery"

Gleaming at sunset, the White Nile joins the Blue Nile at Khartoum, capital of Sudan. Draining the Ethiopian highlands, the 900-mile-long Blue Nile contributes about two-thirds of the water in the main river. More than a thousand miles longer than its sister tributary, the White Nile begins its journey in the mountains of Rwanda and Burundi. The Nile's source waters long eluded discovery.

trickle. In 1937, on a green hillside high in the mountains of present-day Burundi, he found it. A small, insignificant spring becomes the Luvironza River, which flows into the Ruvuvu River, a feeder of the Kagera River. The Kagera empties into Lake Victoria, from which the Nile emerges on its long journey through Uganda, Sudan, and Egypt.

I first saw Nile water at Lake Victoria. It was dusk, and a blood-red sun was poised on rumpled hills far to the west. Hawks swooped past my head, their black eyes watching for a ripple that would mean a fish—and a meal. Waves splashed, and a freshening breeze blew the scent of water to me. For a moment I imagined that I was standing on the shore of an ocean. This enormous freshwater lake is the second largest in the world, after Lake Superior. Measuring roughly 200 miles by 125, it fills a shallow basin between the two arms of the Rift Valley.

Although the water that rippled at my feet belonged to the Nile, I had yet to see the river. For my first look at it, I flew to Khartoum, where the two Niles merge. I arrived in darkness, long past midnight and long before dawn. Near the confluence of the two rivers, I waited, shivering. The sun finally rose and chased away the lingering chill. People stirred in little shacks on the flat floodplain. Men in *jellabiahs*—the flowing robes of North Africa—carried earthenware jugs to the river to draw water. Boys herded shaggy, floppy-eared goats. I walked farther and saw the mingling of the waters of the two Niles. The river to my right, the Blue Nile, had risen in the highlands of Ethiopia, the river to my left, the White Nile, even farther away in Burundi. That dawn in Khartoum, I felt some of the mystery and excitement that had drawn generations of explorers to the eternal Nile.

Two days later I viewed the Nile from a different perspective—as those who live along its banks view it: a giver of life. Flying north down the Nile from Khartoum to Cairo, I could clearly see how the narrow brown band of water nourishes two wider bands of green in the midst of an uncompromising desert. Without the Nile, the Sahara would have complete reign here, as it does elsewhere in North Africa. From the air, the belt of fertility looks vulnerable, transitory. From a boat floating down the Nile, it seems much more permanent. The rich, chocolaty earth yields abundant crops of rice, cotton, sugarcane, and vegetables.

There was a timeless quality to much that I saw along the river.

*V*erdant contrast to the sere slopes on the far bank of the Nile, Elephantine Island near Aswan basks in sunshine. Boatmen paddle a felucca, its sail struck, across the glassy water. A lifeline in the deserts of eastern Africa, the Nile has nurtured civilizations for five thousand years. Farmers once relied on seasonal flooding to irrigate their fields; now dams and canals ensure a year-round water supply. Most of Egypt's 45 million people live in the narrow belt of green bordering the river. The Nile's bounty helps feed the nation. At a market in Luxor, a vendor (opposite) sells fruits and vegetables. In a field near Cairo, a girl balances a load of freshly picked lettuce.

Although modern equipment is widely used, simple machines called shadoofs still draw water from the river and splash it into irrigation ditches. Oxen plow the fields; women wash clothes in the river; and feluccas—the distinctive Nile sailboats—still beat against the wind.

West of Cairo, I stepped from the realm of the Nile to the realm of the Sahara. Where the land has been irrigated, the desert blooms. But the contrast between the two zones is stark—fertile loam becomes shifting sand with little transition. From a knoll in the desert above Cairo, I could gaze down on the living green of the Nile Valley. Just north of the sprawling city lay the delta, a broad fan of productive land. But directly before me was a wasteland, one that holds some of the most enduring monuments ever built: the pyramids of Giza.

As eternal as the Nile is, and as extensively as its waters are used, it greens only 4 percent of Egypt, and Egypt represents less than 10 percent of the Sahara—the largest hot desert on earth. From the Atlantic Ocean to the Red Sea, from the Mediterranean south for a thousand miles, the Sahara controls a vast, virtually uninhabited expanse.

The desert is as diverse as it is colossal. The salt-encrusted Qattara Depression in Egypt drops 436 feet below sea level, while the cold, wind-blown Tibesti Mountains of northern Chad soar to 11,204 feet. There are stretches of dust, regions of rock and gravel, deposits of chalk, gypsum, and other minerals, and long, billowing sand dunes. The Great Sand Sea of Egypt and Libya, for instance, is so enormous that it could hold the state of Virginia.

Dr. Farouk El-Baz, Egyptian-born former director of the Center for Earth and Planetary Studies at the Smithsonian Institution and once science adviser to Egyptian President Anwar Sadat, has mounted a dozen scientific expeditions into the Western Desert—the part of the Sahara in Egypt that lies west of the Nile. Following his advice, I took a short trip to Bahariya Oasis. "Although it's less than 200 miles from Cairo," Farouk said, "you still will get the 'feel' of the desert and what it's like to come upon water and green plants in the midst of barrenness."

"a vast, virtually uninhabited expanse.... as diverse as it is colossal"

Under a sky of cobalt blue, I left the brawl of Cairo in a rented car and drove deep into the desert. I stopped once and walked a few hundred yards across a hard-packed pebbly plain and encountered something Farouk had warned me of: silence. "The silence is so absolute in the desert that some people can't adjust to it. As for me, I luxuriate in it. It's like listening to a perfect musical composition." The only sound I could hear was that of the wind, but so faint I thought I might be imagining it. Even though the air was cool, my mouth felt dry; I was reminded that the Western Desert is one of the most arid places on earth.

After four hours of twisting through a varied landscape of sand and gravel, dune and plain, I came to a hill that dropped away to a broad, flat expanse. Sunlight shimmered here and there on the surfaces of small ponds and illuminated patches of green so brilliant against the sand that they almost hurt my eyes. Bahariya Oasis, like most of the oases in the Sahara, is not a single large pool of water, but rather an extensive depression where water gathers in many places. Some two dozen villages lie scattered throughout the 40-mile-wide depression. I drove slowly into one of them, and my car was immediately swamped by curious, smiling children. They followed me as I walked through narrow streets lined with mud houses to one of the ponds. It nourished neat patches of

vegetables, small fields of grain, grasses for livestock, and large, spreading palms that produce some of the sweetest dates in the world.

That evening, on the way back to Cairo, my car suddenly choked to a halt. As I was opening the hood, a truck drove up and two grinning Egyptians jumped out. Politely, they pushed me aside and began tinkering with the engine. A second truck stopped and then a third. Soon eight of us were crowded around the front of the car, seven Egyptians joking and working and one American smiling and thankful they were there. A moment before sunset, all seven paused, pulled small rugs from their trucks, knelt, and said the ritual Islamic prayers. A little more work and they had solved the problem—a blocked fuel line. I bowed, and stumbled over the few Arabic words of thanks I knew. To have offered payment would have been an insult: I had already learned that when you are in trouble in the desert, everyone is your friend.

Some 2,500 miles beyond the Western Desert, the largely untracked Sahara ends, corralled finally by the only force that could limit it—the ocean. But it ends impressively. In Mauritania, where the Sahara and the Atlantic merge, a 400-mile-long expanse of sand—perhaps the longest continuous sandy beach in the world—ambles north from the Senegal River. Although the Sahara ends, its sands do not. For miles offshore, sandbars and shoals make this coastline one of the most treacherous to navigate in Africa. And in the air, the incessant wind bears a brown blur of dust across the ocean as far as Florida, creating sunsets there that are golden rather than red.

I waded into the booming surf of the blue Atlantic and turned into the wind to face the dun-colored desert. Sahara sand squeezed between my toes, and I tasted grit in my mouth.

After two months of travel in Africa, I had come to appreciate its many moods, its astonishing variety. I thought of Mary Kingsley, a Victorian lady who had ventured into West Africa in the late 1800s. She recognized not only the dangers and the hardships of travel in Africa, but also the enchantment of the land. "And if you do fall under its spell," she wrote, "it takes all the colour out of other kinds of living."

Waves etch packed Sahara sand in Mauritania, where a 400-mile-long stretch of desert—one of the longest continuous sandy beaches in the world—meets the Atlantic Ocean. The Sahara, from an Arabic word meaning "deserts," covers nearly 3½ million square miles and invades ten African nations.

Overleaf: Northerly winds chisel crescent-shaped dunes in Egypt's Western Desert, driest part of the Sahara. Mountains, gravel plains, and salt flats compete with sand in this vast arid wasteland; dune fields cover 20 percent of its surface.

39

Europe

By Ron Fisher
Photographs by
Paul Chesley

Iceland is nature's way of showing off. It's as if nature had decided, in a great burst of experimentation, to try almost everything at least once. In an area the size of Kentucky, there are mountains, rivers, waterfalls, volcanoes, geysers, fjords, mud pools, hot springs, steam holes, new islands, a section of the Mid-Atlantic Ridge, and the largest glacier in Europe.

This geologic exuberance makes Iceland a fitting introduction to the natural wonders of Europe. There's a richness and diversity of wonders on the Continent and adjacent islands that can baffle the hardiest traveler. There's El'brus in the Soviet Union, at 18,510 feet Europe's highest mountain. There are famous rivers whose names resound like struck bells: Danube, Rhine, Seine, Thames, Volga. There are renowned individual peaks: Etna, Vesuvius, Olympus, Jungfrau, Eiger. There are places whose names hint of romance: the Black Forest, the Venetian lagoon, Fingal's Cave. And, for those who think they've seen it all, there's the Rijeka Dubrovačka in Yugoslavia; it's one of the world's largest underground rivers, and it bubbles year round from the base of a limestone cliff into a deep bay.

Of the wonders of Europe, I chose to visit the Norwegian fjords; a strange geologic formation in Northern Ireland; the Alps in France and Switzerland; an ice cave in Austria; a Greek island shaped by a volcanic eruption; and Iceland.

Iceland is unique. An ingenious people has taken this natural wonder and built a nation on top of it. And a proud little nation it is. Icelanders are proud of their island, which perks and simmers like a coffeepot; proud of their Scandinavian language and stirring sagas; and proud of their long democratic tradition.

Iceland straddles the Mid-Atlantic Ridge, a spreading zone between the North American and Eurasian tectonic plates, and thus volcanic activity is fairly common. Molten rock is not far beneath the surface, and on top of that—literally—sit the glaciers. The country is truly a land of ice and fire.

"Heating my home for a month costs about the same as a bottle of whiskey," said Ingvar Fridleifsson. "Of course," he added, "that tells you something about the price of whiskey!"

Dr. Fridleifsson, a geologist with the Icelandic National Energy Authority, drove me around Reykjavík, pointing out the sights of the capital and explaining Iceland's intensive use of the apparently inexhaustible supply of hot water.

"You can tell when the houses in Reykjavík were built just by looking at them," he told me. "Those put up before World War II have chimneys; those built after don't." Why? Because postwar Iceland makes profitable use of the heat trapped underground.

"Geothermal energy supplies a third of this country's total energy

Torrent of meltwater awes two cavers within Kverkjökull, a glacier in Iceland. Heat from a subglacial volcano shaped the icy chamber.

Overleaf: Vatnajökull, Europe's largest ice sheet, mantles a volcano in southeastern Iceland. Meltwater, like a blue island in a calm sea, collects in a depression formed by geothermal activity beneath the ice.

needs," Dr. Fridleifsson said. "About 75 percent of the homes are heated with hot water pumped out of the ground."

He showed me enormous storage tanks, similar to those used for oil, that were full of hot water. "Some of the pipes that carry the water here are so well insulated that the water temperature drops only about one degree in fifteen miles.

"Just to heat the homes of Reykjavík, we pump up to 2,000 liters of water [about 500 gallons] out of the ground every second." Surely at that rate Iceland would soon deplete the supply, I suggested. "Apparently not," he said. "It's constantly replenished by rainfall in the mountains. As the rainwater seeks a path to the sea, it runs underground through thermal areas and is heated. We've been using the hot water since 1930, and there's been no sign of cooling. If we conserve it properly, it should last for centuries."

After leaving Reykjavík, I spent a few days exploring other parts of Iceland, a bizarre country where steam seeps out of the ground, where congealed lava stretches to barren horizons, where melting glaciers nurture frothing rivers.

In *A Journey to the Centre of the Earth*, Jules Verne had his fictional characters begin their descent in Snæfellsjökull, or "snow-mountain glacier," an extinct volcano near Reykjavík. "This benighted island,"

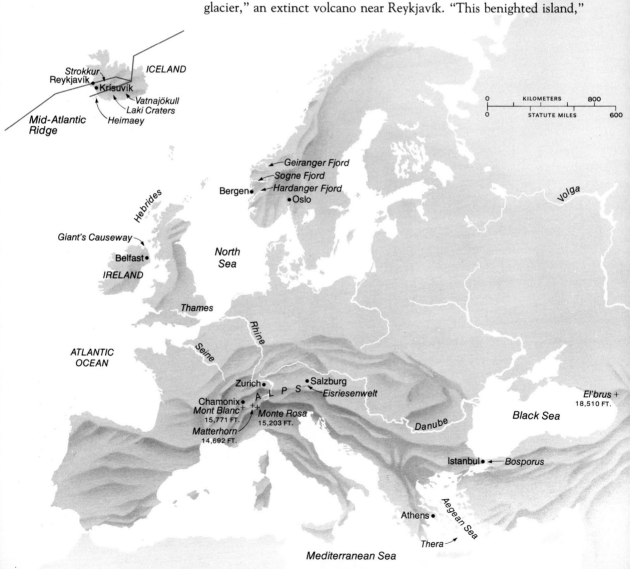

Verne called Iceland, and wrote disparagingly of "meagre pastures," of "a few stunted willows" and "dreary uniformity." His characters saw "spouts of steam rising in the air," and much rough and broken land, the result of "subterraneous commotions."

As I drove on Iceland's rutted gravel roads, sheep alongside them acted as if they'd never seen a car before and bolted for the hills. Shaggy ponies shared the sparse grass with the sheep.

I visited Geysir, which now erupts only a few times a week but was once a gushing fountain that gave us the word "geyser." At a nearby waterfall called Gullfoss—"golden fall"—a sizable river makes two sharp turns, then tumbles into a ravine. Rainbows arch through the clouds of mist above the tumult.

In Krísuvík, a geothermal area south of Reykjavík, plumes of steam appear on the horizon like smoke signals. When a British television crew filmed the witches' scenes in *Macbeth*, they used the bubbling, steaming, sulfurous mud pools at Krísuvík as a location.

In the northeast, miles of brown, cracked lava so resemble a moonscape that American astronauts practiced their Apollo moon mission there. Fences built of lava blocks look fragile and unsubstantial—you can see daylight through them—but the rough chunks of lava cling together so well that the fences have withstood earthquakes for decades.

In the southeast is another wonder: Europe's largest glacier, Vatnajökull. It's really too big to see, covering as it does 3,200 square miles, nearly a tenth of Iceland. It is so massive that if it were spread evenly over the entire island, it would still be nearly 150 feet thick.

From the air this ice sheet shows a blank face that winks and glitters in the sun. Iceland's Highway 1 runs along the southern edge of it, near the coast, and from there I got a closer look. Broad ragged bands of glacier spill around mountains and shed chunks of pale ice that drift seaward on gray streams. Across the flat coastal plain meander dozens of branches and channels; man-made dikes funnel them into single channels to pass beneath bridges. Ducks and geese waddle along the banks. On overcast days, the clouds above Vatnajökull glow with a strange light, as if reflecting fires burning deep in the glacier.

In fact, Vatnajökull sits atop a volcanic zone, and geothermal activity beneath the glacier can produce awesome results. Every few years, water—billions of tons of it, from ice melted by the heat—comes flooding out across the lowlands, sweeping everything before it.

In 1973 a new volcano was born on the island of Heimaey, just off the south coast of Iceland. It erupted for months, practically burying the island's only town in ash and threatening to close the harbor. Workers risked their lives pumping cold water on the lava to harden it and stop its advance, saving the harbor and much of the town.

I made a quick stop on Heimaey to see how the island and the town were faring, and found them better off in some respects than they were before the eruption. The hundreds of tons of volcanic ash have been hauled to other parts of the island and used as landfill on which new homes are rising. The harbor has been improved—made longer and more sheltered. And the Icelanders have even made use of the mountain of still hot lava. More than 300 feet thick in places, the lava will take years to cool, and in the meantime the islanders have built a novel heat-exchange system and buried it in the lava. Water is circulated between the lava and most homes, heating them. The system is expected to

"a richness and diversity of wonders... that can baffle the hardiest traveler"

Europe's jagged outlines enclose a wealth of natural marvels. The majestic Alps arc across the continent's interior, their northern edge pierced by Eisriesenwelt, caverns that include earth's largest known ice cave. In the Caucasus, Europe's highest summit, 18,510-foot Mount El'brus, guards the continent's eastern bounds. Islands hold further wonders: a formidable mix of glaciers and volcanoes on Iceland; the basaltic pillars of the Giant's Causeway in Northern Ireland; and in the Aegean Sea, Thera, survivor of a cataclysm.

remain functional until at least the 1990s, when the lava may be too cool for further use. Heimaey is the only place in the world where hot lava itself is used for fueling a heating system.

Little physical evidence of the eruption remains, except for the lava flow and the new mountain that rests against the edge of town like a sleeping giant. Mosses and buttercups grow along the roads that have been bulldozed through the ash and cinders to the top, and plover eggs lie undisturbed in nests amid cooled lava.

*T*he fjords of Norway were created not by Verne's "subterraneous commotions," but by commotions on the surface: the slow grinding of glaciers as they moved toward the sea. The fjords are justly famous for their grandeur, their wildness, their beauty. Through many centuries of Norwegian history, the fjords performed two functions. On the one hand, they were highways that provided openings to the sea and channels up which foreign influences penetrated Norway. On the other hand, the rugged terrain along the fjords isolated settlements from one another and fostered independence. When Harald Fairhair brought the small kingdoms of Norway under his rule around A.D. 900, the greatest resistance came from the settlers of the fjords. Many resettled in Iceland and other northern European islands.

Hair-raising little highways mosey here and there along Norway's west coast, and where water blocks the way, auto ferries take over. They chug up the fjords, then up arms of the fjords to little towns where hotels, like white leviathans, swallow crowds of tourists.

Cruising through the fjords on the ferries is somewhat like being in a mountain range whose valleys are full of water. Snow-topped mountains slide slowly past, and little islands sprout thick clumps of trees.

Seconds before eruption, a water dome bubbles from Strokkur, one of many Icelandic geysers spouting superheated water. Using geothermal energy to warm his hothouses, Ingimar Sigurdsson of Hveragerdi grows roses for city markets.

Above layers of low clouds the mountains rise to impressive heights. Waterfalls by the dozen—one every mile or so—tumble hundreds of feet in delicate streamers off every mountain.

On Geiranger Fjord—small, remote, and particularly celebrated for its beauty—we passengers sat outside on the top deck in the pale sunlight, except when frequent showers chased us inside to the lounge.

Hardanger Fjord, south of the city of Bergen, is open to mild westerly winds and warm ocean currents, and so it is noted for the extent of its agricultural land and its emerald-green meadows. Farmers' furrows and orchards run in neat rows down slopes to the water's edge.

On a little passenger steamer in Hardanger Fjord, tourists exclaimed as they compared hometowns, but two hours on the freezing boat quieted them. Old ladies clustered around a small electric heater like birds at a feeder. The mountaintops were invisible in the fog.

Sogne Fjord, Norway's longest, reaches inland for more than a hundred miles. Its surface is 3,000 feet below the enclosing plateau, and its floor drops in places to more than 4,000 feet below the sea. Rocky mountains, etched by delicate waterfalls, rise straight up from the shore. I took a daylong excursion up one of the arms of Sogne Fjord to Fjærland, and rode with other tourists through puddles and drizzle to see the countryside. Muddy farms were sprinkled with muddy sheep and muddy farmers driving muddy tractors.

Back on the boat, we felt the day turn colder, with more drizzle and mist. We stopped once in mid-fjord, and a teenage girl stepped from a door in the ship's side into her waiting father's dinghy. Later we stopped again, putting in at a little town to unload a reluctant calf.

In the lounge, a teenage boy was anxiously manipulating a puzzle cube. One woman was busy with her needlepoint, and another with a newspaper. Other tourists were up on deck, dutifully watching the foggy

"congealed lava stretches to barren horizons"

Overleaf: Moss softens the desolation of lava from the Laki craters in southern Iceland. Here in June 1783 began the greatest lava flow of historical times; it lasted for months and buried 220 square miles of farmland. Some 30 active volcanoes ensure at least one eruption in Iceland every two or three years.

mountains slide by. I compromised by staying inside and gazing from a window—at a vista that made me think of trolls.

"Trolls are kind of comic and rather stupid," said Dr. Olav Bø, correcting an impression of mine: I had always pictured trolls as clever little people who lived in tree stumps. But, according to Dr. Bø, who has been associated with the Norwegian Institute for Folklore for 30 years, trolls are giants who live high in the mountains.

When I talked with him in Oslo, he enumerated for me the different kinds of beings that inhabit the Norwegian imagination. And he resolved another puzzle for me by explaining the difference between legends and tales: "Legends are believed; tales are not."

*D*id he believe in trolls when he was young?

"Not in trolls, no, but I was very uncertain about goblins." His thin Viking face crinkled in a smile. Goblins are hill people, too, but smaller than giants. "Our Norwegian giants are friendlier than those in most other countries," he said. "In many lands the giants are symbols of the evil forces in nature. But Norwegian giants are so dull-witted that it's not difficult for the young heroes of the tales to outsmart them. It's interesting that, in Norway, the larger the creature, the less dangerous he is. Trolls and other giants are harmless."

I asked Dr. Bø about the connection between Norway's rich folklore and its distinctive landscape. "Many features are attributed to the work of the giants," he said. "For instance, in the north there is a coastal mountain with a hole through it—right through it. Of course, the sea must have once reached that level and made the hole, but a tale blames it on a giant. He was chasing a beautiful giantess, and when he realized he couldn't catch her, he fired an arrow after her. The arrow made the hole." Another tale explains the presence of a large canyon. Two trolls were fighting, one threw down his ax, and presto!—a canyon.

Another giant, this time an Irish one, was responsible for a geologic marvel on the coast of Northern Ireland. The Giant's Causeway, according to Irish folklore, marks the beginning of a road built by Finn McCool across the channel from Ireland to Staffa, an island in Scotland's Hebrides, where a similar formation—Fingal's Cave—occurs. Indeed, the Causeway looks more man-made than any other geologic formation I have ever seen. Lines by an early 19th-century Irish poet, W. H. Drummond, make the same point:

> *A far projecting, firm, basaltic way*
> *Of clustering columns wedged in dense array;*
> *. . . reason pauses, doubtful if it stand*
> *The work of mortal, or immortal hand.*

Some 37,000 basaltic columns, cheek by jowl, rise 20 feet or more out of the ground. Each is one or two feet wide and has from three to nine sides. Legend notwithstanding, the formation was born of molten lava millions of years ago. As the lava cooled, it formed these many-sided pillars. The Causeway covers about five acres. In nearby cliffs are more columns, some of them 40 feet high.

To reach the Causeway, I drove from Belfast northward along the coast of Northern Ireland through exquisite countryside. On my right, the sea lapped at rocky beaches and hurled clouds of spray landward. Inland, patchwork fields of every shade of green blanketed rolling hills.

"like being in a mountain range whose valleys are full of water"

Wooded cliffs plunge to the water's edge along Norway's Geiranger Fjord. Snowmelt from mountains high above feeds streaming waterfalls; the intertwining Seven Sisters tumbles near a passing ferry. Long fingers of the sea, fjords penetrate much of the country's coastline, providing, in the words of one Norwegian writer, a "road between friends."

Mountain fastness cradles a family farm above Geiranger Fjord. Harvesters stack hay on wood-and-wire frames to dry. In summer, tourists invade this isolated area, swelling the population of the village at the end of the small fjord. Glaciers account for much of Norway's beauty, nurturing frothy waterfalls and, in ages past, carving fjords from the mountains. At Briksdal (opposite, lower), glacial runoff spills down a mountainside; a horse-drawn buggy carries visitors to view part of Jostedalsbre, Norway's largest glacier. Opposite, upper: Sustained by the sea, Anders Bjåstad has spent his life as a sailor and fisherman. Now retired, he still fishes in an arm of Sogne Fjord near his home.

Thick lines of gorse, in vibrant yellow bloom, marked fence rows, and fluffy white sheep gamboled and frolicked in the green fields. Gray clouds sailed by overhead.

I remarked to an Irish girl, "It's supposed to rain today, the radio said." "It says that every day," she answered.

Ages ago, some of the columns at the Causeway split horizontally, creating a sort of ball-and-socket joint at each fracture. Local lore says that peasants of the 17th and 18th centuries filled the exposed sockets with seawater, waited a few days until it had evaporated, then collected the salt that was left behind.

Descriptions and drawings of the Causeway began to circulate in the 18th century, creating a good deal of speculation and interest. But not universally. James Boswell tried to interest Dr. Samuel Johnson in a trip to Ireland, but Johnson was reluctant. Boswell asked if he didn't think the Giant's Causeway worth seeing. "Worth seeing? Yes; but not worth going to see."

Not everyone who visited the Causeway liked the experience. Novelist William Makepeace Thackeray, a Cockney, came in 1845 but was put off by the wild and rugged countryside and wished he was home: "The solitude is awful. . . . It looks like the beginning of the world, somehow: the sea looks older than in other places, the hills and rocks strange. . . . When the world was moulded and fashioned out of formless chaos, this must have been the *bit over*—a remnant of chaos! . . . I wish I were in Pall Mall!"

But Mrs. Delany, wife of the Bishop of Down, thought the Causeway was "the most wonderful sight that perhaps is to be seen in the world." And the Chevalier de Latocnaye of France enjoyed his trip along the coast, as did his horse. The animal "seemed to joy in the beauty of the scene, approaching to the edge of the precipice and letting his eye range the horizon with a look of admiration."

Everyone complained of the swarms of aggressive guides who offered their services to visitors. In the late 19th century the Causeway was fenced in and admission charged. The land was acquired by Britain's National Trust in 1961; today admission is free.

Jackdaws and gulls wheeled and squalled overhead while I was there, and two workmen with a wheelbarrow were repairing the footpath. Except for them I was alone, a rare circumstance indeed at one of nature's more accessible wonders.

A wonder of nature, by its nature, attracts the wondering, and in Switzerland, next on my itinerary, the tourists were out in force. I include myself among them. I love being a tourist and join in wholeheartedly. I wear sensible shoes and make sure I have plenty of film. I buy souvenirs and postcards for my friends and shop endlessly, comparing bargains with my fellow pilgrims.

We are a hardy bunch. We dutifully line up and wait our turns; we suffer rudeness and confusion placidly; we complain of our aching feet but seldom of the food. Late in the day we begin to sag. Our responses grow a little perfunctory: "Lovely, isn't it?" "Lovely."

Nothing—not all the descriptions I had read, not all the photographs I had seen—quite prepared me for the size and splendor of the Alps. Above the heart-stopping switchbacks, the snowy summits rise to enormous heights. Tidy farms cling to steep slopes like grassy barnacles.

" 'a remnant of chaos' "

Stepping-stones for a giant, basaltic columns mass along the coast of Northern Ireland. Local tradition holds that legendary hero Finn McCool planned the Giant's Causeway as a bridge across the North Channel to Scotland. Geologists explain that an ancient lava bed cooled, contracted, and fractured into these many-sided pillars filling five acres.

LINDA BARTLETT/WOODFIN CAMP & ASSOCIATES

The complex geologic structure of the Alps has been studied intensively since the second half of the 19th century, when geology began to gain respectability as a legitimate science, especially in Europe. Geologists, however, still disagree about the origin of these mountains. Most now cite the theory of plate tectonics: As the African plate moved slowly northward against the more stable European landmass, the original area of the Alps was compressed by as much as 300 miles. This great upheaval, which started some 25 million years ago, created huge, complex folds—called nappes—in the thick sedimentary rock. Young nappes were sometimes overlaid by older ones or even turned upside down. Other geologists say that the older material on top was thrust up through breaks in the younger. Whatever happened, it seems that some of the younger mountains are still rising, edging slowly upward even as erosion works to wear them down.

South of Zurich I ran afoul of a late spring: One of the many passes through the Alps was closed by snow, which sent me backtracking. I stopped for the night at the William Tell Hotel in a little village, along with what seemed to be most of the Swiss Army. Hundreds of officers and men had taken over the village during their maneuvers, and the one street was full of polite and happy soldiers. On my bed that night was a feather comforter five feet square and a foot thick.

I arrived in the town of Zermatt by train, like everyone else. No cars are allowed here, and little electric trucks and horse-drawn cabs carry the tourists from the station to their hotels. The Matterhorn, one of the most famous sights in Europe, looms above the town, just as it does in photographs. I was not the first person to notice this. Mark Twain wrote in his travel book, *A Tramp Abroad:* "We were approaching Zermatt; consequently, we were approaching the renowned Matterhorn. A month before, this mountain had been only a name to us, but latterly we had been moving through a steadily thickening double row of pictures of it, done in oil, water, chromo, wood, steel, copper, crayon, and photography. . . .

"Think of a monument a mile high, standing on a pedestal two miles high!" Twain went on. "This is what the Matterhorn is—a monument." Indeed it is an impressive mountain, and has attracted millions of visitors, many of them climbers.

The Alpine climber I find the most interesting never made it to the top of the Matterhorn, but she—yes, she—climbed most of the other famous peaks between 1865 and 1876. She was a dog—yes, a dog—named Tschingel, that made 66 major climbs and 100 minor ones with her American-born owner, the Rev. W.A.B. Coolidge. "Although brought up to respond to Swiss-German," according to a chronicler of Alpine climbers, "she quickly learned English, but never responded to French, a trait that her master put down to annoyance with the arduous journey across France caused by the outbreak of the Franco-Prussian war."

When this intrepid hound went climbing, her favorite drinks were red wine and cold tea. She was troubled by bleeding paws, so Coolidge made leather boots for her, but she pulled them off. Sometimes, at high elevations, the tip of her nose became sunburned. Evidently these problems didn't detract from her enjoyment of climbing.

In 1869 she climbed Monte Rosa, on the Swiss-Italian border, and
was rewarded with honorary membership in the prestigious Alpine

Club. On July 24, 1875, she made her finest climb, the first unassisted canine ascent of Mont Blanc. An admiring crowd awaited her in Chamonix, at the base, and "she trotted into the village with her head erect and her tail wagging, immensely proud of herself." On special occasions, Tschingel wore a collar with silver medallions commemorating her climbs. She died in her sleep in 1879, at the ripe old age of 15.

To reach the site of Tschingel's most famous climb—Mont Blanc—I drove just over the border into France, to Chamonix. Again Mark Twain had been here before me. "We hired a sort of open baggage-wagon for the trip down the valley to Chamonix, and then devoted an hour to dining. This gave the driver time to get drunk."

Here, too, among "savage and enduring scenes," had wandered Mary Shelley's despondent Dr. Frankenstein: "The immense mountains and precipices that overhung me on every side, the sound of the river raging among the rocks, and the dashing of the waterfalls around spoke of a power mighty as Omnipotence. . . ." He ascended higher up the valley of the Arve River and the "singular beauty" of the scene "was augmented and rendered sublime by the mighty Alps, whose white and shining pyramids and domes towered above all, as belonging to another earth, the habitations of another race of beings." Finally he reached a place where he could see "Mont Blanc, in aweful majesty," a "wonderful and stupendous scene."

Stupendous, indeed. The Matterhorn may be more impressive, but Mont Blanc is, I think, more beautiful. At 15,771 feet, it is the highest mountain in the Alps, beating out Monte Rosa by some 500 feet.

The day I arrived, clouds and snow collaborated to transform Mont Blanc into a white, shifting mass that loomed over Chamonix like another separate world. In the streets of the town I heard a polyglot of Europe's languages—French, German, English.

Chamonix shuts down between noon and 2:30 p.m. Most shops close, and the high hot sun beats down on streets emptied of everyone but footsore tourists, who gaze with longing into the windows of shuttered, air-conditioned shops.

It was here that I noticed that wonders of nature can begin to pall, that the senses will only absorb so much grandeur before they rebel. In the cable gondola swaying slowly toward the top of the spectacular Aiguille du Midi, below the summit of Mont Blanc, I heard a middle-aged tourist, very tired, muse aloud to her camera-toting husband: "They say mini-skirts are coming back."

The top of the Aiguille was rocky, snowy, icy, and cloudy, chilly but not cold, and tourists happily snapped pictures of one another with Mont Blanc in the background. Little black specks in the distance were climbers approaching the top. Marmots played in the snow beneath the gondola as we descended, and we glimpsed a couple of deer far below among the dense trees.

No trees—virtually no vegetation at all—grow in one of nature's coldest wonders, an ice cave on the northern rim of the Alps near Salzburg, in Austria. Eisriesenwelt—"world of the ice giants"—is touted as earth's largest ice cave, and to reach it you travel up. And up. And up.

I drove south from Salzburg to Werfen, where I parked my car and boarded a Volkswagen bus with four English and four Austrian tourists. In low gear we crawled four miles up the side of the Hochkogel, around hairpin turns and alongside nonexistent shoulders where the mountain dropped away beneath us.

" 'the mighty Alps... belonging to another earth, the habitations of another race of beings' "

Overleaf: On a pathway through the sky, cable gondolas carrying passengers between Chamonix, in France, and Courmayeur, in Italy, offer sweeping vistas of the Alps. The celebrated mountains bestow their lofty splendors on seven European countries and attract skiers and climbers from around the world.

The driver let us off at a parking lot 1,500 feet above the valley floor. From there we walked for 15 minutes farther up the mountain on a narrow gravel road to a hut where we boarded an aerial cable car for a nearly perpendicular five-minute ride still farther up the mountain. We got off the cable car at another hut. From there it was a 15-minute walk up a narrow path to the mouth of the cave.

There was a restaurant in the second hut, and one waitress— the busiest I ever saw—was trying to serve a hundred people at the same time. I sat outside in the warm sun and enjoyed a breathtaking Alpine view, as yellow-eyed ravens swooped and darted and snatched tidbits thrown them by the tourists. A group of Austrian schoolboys, waiting to tour the cave, eddied about me like surf.

At the mouth of the cave, we formed an orderly line and then filed slowly into a hole 60 feet across in the side of the mountain. There are no electric lights in the cave, so our young guide gave every tenth person a little carbide lamp that burned with a lovely, soft glow. We made quite a picture as we set off in single file along the wooden boardwalk and up the wooden steps.

Eisriesenwelt was formed by water seeping down through cracks in the limestone of the mountain. The water dissolved the soft rock, leaving a system of caves that honeycomb the mountain for 26 miles. Because of the low temperatures inside the cave, water seeping into some of the passages freezes and stays frozen year round.

Beside us, as we made our way through the darkness, wondrous icy shapes appeared. They glittered and pulsed as our lamps shone through and around them. We climbed the glistening slope of a huge bed of ice that curved through the passageways. We passed formations like those in other caves—stalagmites and stalactites—but these were made of ice.

Our guide carried a magnesium flare, and whenever we came to an especially interesting spot, he would light it, flooding the cave with bright but mellow beams. As he spoke, the cloud of his condensing breath mingled with the smoke from the flare, obscuring him in mist.

He told us the history of the cave as we went along. It was discovered in 1879 by Anton von Posselt-Czorich, who got as far as 600 feet into it. Some 30 years later the man whose name is most closely associated with the cave visited it for the first time. Alexander von Mörk, an accomplished Austrian speleologist, led several expeditions into the cave in 1912 and 1913, and named it. In those days it took six or seven hours of climbing just to reach the mouth. It wasn't until 1920 that paths were completed up the mountain, and the cave was opened to visitors.

Meanwhile, von Mörk had been killed in World War I. An urn containing his ashes sits on a frost-covered rock ledge in a sort of memorial niche within the cave.

Bringing up the rear of our little train were the oldest members of the group. They had quite a time. They would get left in the dark as the people in front of them carrying the lamps rounded corners. You could hear them back there, squealing and laughing as they groped their way, slipping and sliding, through the inky blackness. Their good humor and robustness impressed me. Back in the sunshine at the hut, one of the older women, a grandmotherly sort, plopped onto a bench in the shade, fanned herself with her skirt, and quaffed a glass of cold beer as if she were afraid it might be her last.

Eisriesenwelt—"world of the ice giants"—winks and gleams as lanterns help dispel the darkness. Fanciful formations such as the Eistor—"ice door" (below)—line the passageways of this immense ice cave, deep in the Austrian Alps. Water seeping through

the cavern's porous limestone freezes into an array of ice stalactites, stalagmites, domes, and towers. High in the northern Alps' Tennengebirge range, a narrow path (opposite, upper) switchbacks up the Hochkogel to the cave entrance. Just inside the mouth, a guide (opposite, lower) lights carbide lamps before taking visitors on a tour through sections of Eisriesenwelt's subterranean wonderland.

Having survived Eisriesenwelt, I journeyed to Greece and boarded a ferry to Thera, a little island in the Aegean Sea some 130 miles from Piraeus, the port serving Athens. I ventured out onto the cold and windy deck, where hardy Germans in shorts leaned against their backpacks, their knees pink from the cold. After a 12-hour trip, we reached Thera at dusk, just as a full moon was rising. Another name for the island—Santorini—is a contraction of Santa Irene, its patron saint. Thera lies in the Cyclades group of islands; it is also one of the volcanic islands that stretch in an arc between Greece and Asia Minor.

Thera is an unusual site: the place where a wonder of nature destroyed a wonder of man. Thirty-five centuries ago, a volcanic eruption occurred in the center of Thera. The cone collapsed inward, leaving a crescent-shaped island. In the bay created by the eruption, more recent volcanic activity has created smaller islands. One of them still steams continually, betraying the presence of molten lava far below. In places the harbor is 1,300 feet deep, too deep for ships to anchor; they tie up to lines stretched out from shore.

The eruption, which affected life on islands nearly a hundred miles away, may have changed the course of Minoan civilization. On Thera itself, dust and ash buried the Minoan town of Akrotiri. It remained buried until 1967, when Spyridon Marinatos, then Inspector General of Antiquities for Greece, began excavations.

The major excavation has been covered by an enormous shed to protect it from further weathering, and it is a cool and spooky place. A shaggy dog with a wagging tail greeted me at the entrance. Inside,

Tourists on donkeyback make their way up from the harbor to a cliffside town on Thera. Thirty-five centuries ago a volcanic eruption overwhelmed the Aegean island with such violence that debris rained down on much of the eastern Mediterranean.

N.G.S. PHOTOGRAPHER JAMES P. BLAIR

clumps of grass have sprouted in the dirt beneath leaks in the roof. Birds chirp in the rafters, and flies buzz among the dusty ruins. Streets and buildings and public squares have been cleared of rubble, but it was difficult for me to imagine people living here: Everything seemed slightly smaller than life—tiny windows, low roofs, narrow streets.

Peaceful Akrotiri contrasts dramatically with the noisy, bustling tourist center a few miles away in the town of Thera, where woebegone little donkeys carry tourists up the steep cliff from the dock. People who choose to ride arrive at the top looking slightly shamefaced. Those who take pity on the donkeys and elect to walk arrive panting and red-faced from the effort.

Sleek taxis and lumbering buses compete for space on narrow roads, and goats disdainfully watch the traffic go by. The stone towers of crumbling windmills—not used since the coming of "the electric" to Thera many years ago—dot the horizon.

On the very top of Mount Prophetes Elias, at 1,857 feet the highest point on the island, sits a monastery built in 1711. With a small group, I stopped in for a visit. A shy, grinning gatekeeper, who spoke no English, tried to make a tourist in shorts, who spoke no Greek, understand that he was to put on a robe to cover his bare legs. A small chapel near the entrance was filled to overflowing with ornate reliquaries, antique censers, and religious paintings.

For 35 drachmas (about 40 cents), we entered the museum, where almost every aspect of the monastery's life was displayed. There were rooms devoted to wine making, bread baking, linen and rug weaving, and agriculture. The monastery was a warren of low archways, narrow stone stairways, and tiny whitewashed rooms that included a barbershop, a library, a bindery, and a kitchen. Bearded monks in black robes could be glimpsed going about their business along dim corridors.

From the monastery, I set off down the mountain. Dozens of tiny lizards were panicked by my clodhopper descent. Daisies and buttercups bloomed along the path, and the sea lapped at golden beaches far below me. Grumpy black bees thumped against my arms, but didn't sting.

A 45-minute walk brought me to a parking lot where another path led upward to "Old Thera," a town built by Dorians in the eighth century B.C. The site was excavated by a German archaeologist, Hiller von Gaetringen, between 1895 and 1903.

Unlike the ruins of Akrotiri, the toppled columns and tilting walls here have been left exposed to the elements, and grass and wild flowers grow among them. I could easily imagine people living in this place, in the bright sunshine and the fresh air, with the land dropping down toward the blue Aegean.

My last afternoon on Thera, I sat at the outdoor café of my hotel, just a few yards from the beach, and watched the passing scene. A black cocker spaniel sat beside me in the benign Aegean sun. A low-slung freighter steamed slowly by, a mile out at sea.

Leaving the natural wonders of Europe behind, I arrived a few days later in Istanbul, in Turkey. The teeming city sprawls on the banks of the Bosporus, traditional dividing line between two continents. Armed soldiers patrolled the noisy streets, and lilacs bloomed in the hotel courtyard. A ragged shoeshine boy, walking along talking to himself, looked not at my face as he approached, but at my shoes. Deliverymen hurried down crowded sidewalks, Turkish carpets slung over their shoulders. Ships' horns hooted mournfully on the Bosporus, and across the narrow strait, dimly seen through the early morning mist, were the minarets and the red tile roofs of Asia.

Another world of wonders awaited me there.

"the place where a wonder of nature destroyed a wonder of man"

Overleaf: Whitewashed town hugs Thera's crescent-shaped coast. The deep bay beyond fills a caldera created when a volcanic cone erupted, then collapsed. More recent eruptions have formed smaller islands in the bay. Volcanic activity may eventually reclaim the area lost to the sea.

GORDON W. GAHAN

Asia

By Ron Fisher

I awoke in darkness, disoriented, to the sound of little bells ringing and with someone tugging on my foot. A voice murmured, "Five minutes till sunrise, sir, and it's fine." I remembered where I was: high on the flank of Mount Fuji in Japan. I crawled out from under my heavy quilt, found my boots, and went outside into the cold dawn. To the east, thin clouds were turning pink and gold across the horizon. The valley at the foot of Fuji still lay in darkness, but shapes—lakes and hills—were emerging from the heavy blanket of mist.

I munched on an apple and a piece of cheese and watched as the sun edged above the horizon—a gradual explosion of light that bathed me in a warming glow.

The night before, along with several hundred other climbers, I had set out on an ascent of Fuji, one of the most famous and widely recognized mountains in the world. Its symmetrical cone has become, in the minds of many, a perfect emblem of Japan.

A dormant volcano, Mount Fuji looms large not only in the Japanese landscape, but also in the Japanese imagination. For centuries it has been a sacred mountain, the frequent subject of poets and painters. Just below the summit is a Shinto shrine erected nearly 2,000 years ago by the Emperor Suinin in an attempt to placate the mountain, which was erupting at the time. The first recorded eruption of Fuji occurred in A.D. 800, and the most recent, in 1707—a powerful blast that dropped ash and cinders on Tokyo, more than 60 miles away.

Mount Fuji was the first stop on my 5,000-mile swing across Asia, world enough for any wonder seeker to lose himself in. Nature works her wonders on a grand scale here, thrusting up lofty mountains, then whittling away at them. There are mountains born of fire—like Fuji—and others born of the slow collision of the earth's crustal plates—like the Himalayas. Rivers such as the Yangtze (Chang Jiang) and the Ganges move mountains to create awesome natural spectacles. And on the Japanese island of Kyūshū, subterranean volcanism keeps the surface bubbling and steaming.

At 12,388 feet, Fuji is the highest mountain in Japan. Its base is an almost perfect circle 25 miles across. Today a doughnut of development rings the mountain, for Fuji is the centerpiece of a large and popular national park. So popular, in fact, that it is nearly overrun by visitors. Some 400,000 people climb Fuji each year, virtually all of them during the short climbing season in July and August.

Many Japanese climb Fuji at night to be at or near the summit for sunrise. So I was right on schedule when a bus from Tokyo let me off at the fifth of ten stages on the flank of the mountain about 10:30 one warm summer night. Lights burned in a couple of souvenir shops and restaurants, and the parking lots were full of Toyotas and Hondas, but most of the climbers had already started up.

"Glorious sea, sacred Baykal," extolled in an old Russian song, gleams below snowy cliffs in Siberia. The world's deepest lake, Baykal catches the flow of 330 rivers and holds a fifth of the earth's fresh water.

Overleaf: Mount Fuji reigns as Japan's loftiest and holiest peak. "Be pure. . . . Stay fair, O ye mountain!" pilgrims chant on the way to the summit.

A broad graveled path disappeared upward into darkness. I shouldered my little pack, bulging with a jacket, snacks, a canteen of water, and a flashlight, and set out.

In the light of a full moon, trees and boulders cast black shadows, and heavily wooded areas were pitch dark. As I climbed out of the woods, I could see above and below me on the trail the beams from hundreds of flashlights as other climbers gradually made their way up the mountain. Many carried walking sticks with little bells attached. So with lights bobbing and bells tinkling, we moved upward through the night. I remembered an old Japanese haiku: "O snail, climb Mount Fuji. But slowly. Slowly."

About two o'clock in the morning, as the trail began switchbacking steeply through a landscape of volcanic debris—boulders and rocks and gravel—I came to several small stone huts offering tea and shelter. I stopped in one run by five teenage boys in kimonos and sandals. In the center of the wooden floor an enormous teakettle hung over a fire pit. Along one wall a shelf wide enough to accommodate mattresses held several climbers already asleep. After a cup of green tea and a little rudimentary conversation, I turned in, only to be awakened all too soon by the tug at my foot and the sound of little bells ringing.

When the mist cleared, I gazed at the unforgettable sweep of green hills and placid lakes in Fuji-Hakone-Izu National Park. After the sun was well up, I turned away reluctantly and started down. Still the trail was thick with people ascending and descending. Back at stage five I encountered a weekend-at-Disneyland atmosphere. Buses were disgorging tourists by the score. Hawkers offered pony rides and hot dogs, and amplified pop music competed with transistor radios.

Southwest of Fuji, on the northeast coast of the island of Kyūshū, the little city of Beppu curves around the gentle scallop of Beppu Bay. Two ancient volcanoes—Mount Tsurumi and Mount Yufu—rise behind the city like green-cloaked giants. From above, Beppu looks as though it's under bombardment, for plumes of smokelike steam waft from dozens of spots throughout the city.

Beppu sits on top of a thermal area that burns and hisses just 800 feet below the surface. Each day ten million gallons of hot water come pouring out of 3,000 hot springs, and the Japanese arrive en masse to soak in the steaming, smelly waters.

Taking the waters is a tradition in Japan that began many centuries ago, most likely in Buddhist purification rites. Buddhist priests also began treating ailments with regimens of bathing in the hot springs. Today the Japanese probably lead the world in the use of natural hot water in baths, therapeutic spas, and resorts.

An eruption of Mount Tsurumi in 867 started the hot waters of Beppu flowing, and they show no sign of stopping. More than 800 hotels and other lodgings welcome the flood of visitors, who can choose among several different kinds of hot springs: Alkali springs are said to heal burns and skin diseases; sulfur springs improve the circulation; and carbonic springs alleviate stomach troubles. Other visitors bury themselves to the chin in *sunayus*—hot sand beaches that give comfort to sufferers from arthritis.

I checked into a 3,000-room resort hotel whose two giant pools— each capable of holding 1,000 people—were filled with bathers. The pool areas were virtual jungles, with lush greenery and ornate statuary

Largest of the seven continents, Asia claims nearly a third of the world's land. Asia's natural wonders run to superlatives. More than 60 peaks in the Himalayan and the Karakoram ranges stand higher than any on the other continents. Several of the world's major rivers—including the Yangtze in China and the Ganges on the Indian subcontinent— water Asian lands. From Mount Fuji to Krakatau, volcanism helped shape the region's islands.

fringing bays and inlets. The hotel hallways, shopping arcades, bowling alley, restaurants, and amusement centers swarmed with guests wearing identical kimonos and slippers supplied by the hotel.

The Japanese have always known how best to utilize the limited natural resources of their country. As long ago as 1924, when a single kilowatt of electricity was generated by a hot spring at Beppu, scientists were studying ways of harnessing thermal energy here. Today the town gets much of its energy from the hot springs. The hotels, for instance, are heated by steam piped from the springs. And wells have been drilled to capture the steam so that it can be used in generating electricity. Beppu, say thermal engineers, is capable of producing 40 million kilowatts a year for the next thousand years.

In Japan, bells on walking sticks awoke me, but in Guilin, in China, I awoke to the sound of bicycle bells. Below my hotel window, the wide boulevard running through Guilin was thronged with early morning cyclists pedaling sedately to work. City buses, packed to the doorways, wove through the crowd, (Continued on page 80)

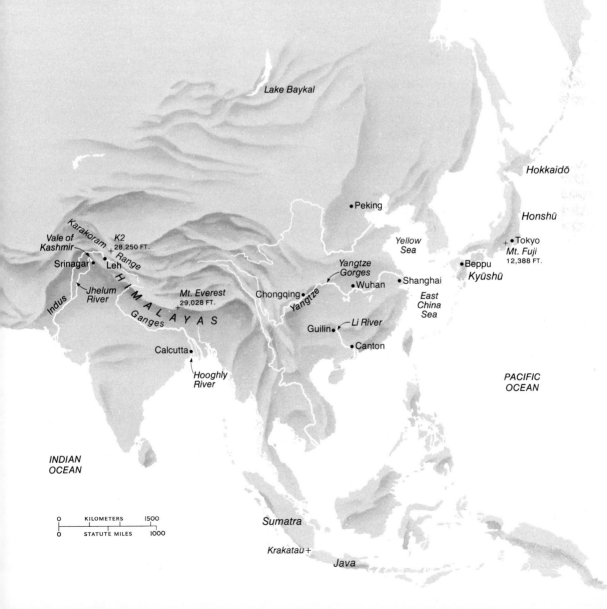

*B*eneath a gilded statue of Buddha, guests luxuriate in thermal waters at an elaborate bathhouse at Beppu, in Japan. Here on the island of Kyūshū, nearly 4,000 hot springs yield thousands of gallons daily—nine different kinds of mineral waters bubbling out of the ground at varying temperatures. Opposite: Hikers on the northern island of Hokkaidō soak in their own natural hot tub.

Overleaf: At dawn, steam from the earth wafts toward a small pagoda near Beppu. The Japanese tradition of bathing perhaps originated in Buddhist cleansing rituals. Now millions of people come to Beppu yearly for therapeutic treatment or for relaxation.

PAUL CHESLEY (ABOVE); MICHAEL S. YAMASHITA

horns blaring. Pedestrians—the men in shorts and undershirts, the women in baggy trousers and jackets—scurried by. Many carried loads on their backs or in baskets dangling from poles across their shoulders. Cassia trees grew in profusion along the sidewalks; they gave the city its name, for Guilin translates as "cassia forest." In the Li River, bathers performed their morning ablutions. And across the river rose the rounded pinnacles of limestone, called tower karst, that make Guilin famous.

"A thousand seas poured into one cup," a poet described the Yangtze River in its narrow gorges. Sails trimmed, a sampan passes beneath precipitous walls. Third longest river in the world, after the Nile and the Amazon, the Yangtze courses nearly 4,000 miles across central China. Crews once risked their lives towing boats upstream over roiling rapids. Today giant winches do the job.

It's a landscape you may have seen in Chinese paintings. Beyond a quiet scene—perhaps a peasant climbing toward a shrine, or a fisherman casting his net across a lake—rise steep hills shrouded in mist and green with trees. Ever higher and fainter, they recede into the dim distance. This landscape is the Guilin karst. The hills were formed by the slow erosion of an ancient, uplifted limestone seabed. They are riddled with caves, and they reach right into the center of Guilin.

Guilin is an old city, first settled in 214 B.C. during construction of a canal that tied the Yangtze River Basin to the Canton (Guangzhou) area via the Li River. In 1664 the Ming emperor and his court moved to Guilin to escape the Manchus, who had captured Peking (Beijing). During World War II, Guilin was the headquarters of the Flying Tigers, the American Volunteer Group organized in 1941 to assist China in its struggle against Japan. Heavy bombing by the Japanese caused severe damage, and when the Japanese advanced on the city, the airbase there was deliberately destroyed by the retreating Americans.

I spent several days in the Guilin area, being shown around with a busload of other tourists. Our local guide, Fong Paomin—"You call me Mr. Fong"—had a happy smile and dimples, and he shepherded us through the sweltering countryside with patience and good humor. Mopping our brows, we trudged up the 440 steps to the top of one of the karst hills on the outskirts of the city. Guilin sprawled below us, peaceful along the banks of the Li. Haze made the hills appear ghostly and even more bizarre, magical things that a child might build.

We visited a famous cave in one of the hills. Mr. Fong lectured us at the entrance: "Why is the name called Reed Flute Cave? The name is called Reed Flute Cave because. . . ."

Because of the reeds that once concealed the entrance and that made fine flutes, according to local lore. Inside, fanciful stone figures had been given fanciful names, and colored lights played over them. A huge grotto, the Crystal Palace, could have held a thousand people comfortably, and indeed once did. Many Chinese took refuge in the caves during the bombings of World War II.

Another day we stopped at a "free market," an experiment in free enterprise that the authorities permit. In a large shed, local farmers had come to sell their amazingly varied produce. It was hot and noisy in the crowded market, and flies buzzed in the thick, humid air. Ducks, their wings broken so they couldn't fly, waddled beneath long wooden tables. A bundle of frogs, their hind legs all tied together, wriggled in a bucket. Shoppers picked over mounds of vegetables and fruits. Baby chicks peeped in bamboo crates. One of the vendors had a frisky puppy on a string, and another had a trained mouse that spun a wheel with single-minded determination. Turtles napped on the dusty floor.

The next day we drove for several hours through the countryside in our little bus. The highways were practically empty of vehicles, but crowded with people—hardy peasants carrying loads of vegetables, baskets of rice, bundles of firewood, even pigs. Brick houses the color of earth squatted alongside the roads. Fields of plump watermelons grew in the valleys, and scarecrows—many of them elaborate creatures dressed in ragged but matching ensembles—stood guard in rice fields.

"the river narrowed dramatically as it squeezed between two peaks"

We boarded a launch on the Li River for a six-hour cruise through the heart of the karst country. The Chinese themselves say that this is probably the most beautiful spot in China.

The green-clad hills rose like phantoms along the busy river. Swimming children shared the shallows with water buffaloes submerged to their eyebrows. Narrow bamboo rafts plied the caramel-colored river. On one sat a row of big black cormorants, like sailors lined up for inspection. Fishermen train the birds to dive for fish; strings tied around their necks prevent them from swallowing all but the smallest fish. Farmers on the banks waved as we passed their villages of brick houses tucked among shade trees.

Many of the Chinese I met were eager to practice their English. It was a rare hotel or restaurant that didn't have at least one staff member who would ask for an English lesson. Once a little group of waiters and waitresses clustered around me as I ate, to talk and to sing "Jingle Bells"—this in August, with fans whispering overhead and flowers drooping in the heat.

If I was interested in the Chinese people, they were fascinated by me. I tried to stroll through a crowded village marketplace and was immediately surrounded by 500 curious Chinese, who stood and stared at my bearded face as if they had never expected to see such a sight. When I was taken to view the pandas in the zoo at Kunming, I drew twice the crowd the pandas did.

At Chongqing I boarded a large cruise ship with several hundred Chinese and a handful of tourists for a trip through another scenic wonder of China: the Yangtze River Gorges.

*M*orning mist on the Li River transforms the karst landscape of Guilin, China, into a poet's "hills of jade." Millions of years ago, a seabed was uplifted, then became eroded, leaving these limestone pinnacles that have long inspired China's artists. Lantern in hand, a cormorant fisherman sets out at sunrise. When his birds dive for fish, a noose keeps them from swallowing any but the smallest catch. Opposite: Pagodas grace the summit of a tower karst formation.

The third longest river in the world, after the Nile and the Amazon, the Yangtze flows for nearly 4,000 miles from mountains in Tibet to the East China Sea. The river drains 695,000 square miles and touches the lives of 300 million Chinese. In the last 2,000 years, the Yangtze has flooded 1,500 times. Disastrous floods along its lower reaches in 1931 killed 145,000 people and displaced 28 million more.

The Yangtze is China's great central thoroughfare, linking east and west, and historically it has served as a principal artery of conquest as well as commerce. During the days of "gunboat diplomacy" in the 19th and early 20th centuries, foreign steam vessels cruised up and down the Yangtze attempting to keep the peace and protect various commercial interests. Today the river carries at least two-thirds of all the goods shipped on China's inland waterways.

As it enters the final quarter of its journey, the Yangtze passes through 127 miles of spectacular gorges, and it was to see them that I boarded the ship for a three-day voyage between Chongqing and Wuhan. The Chinese passengers traveling between cities were packed onto the lower decks, but we tourists were assigned a deck of our own.

So that we might travel through the gorges in daylight, we docked at Wanxian for the night, and I went ashore for a walk after dinner. The streets were crowded with strollers and shoppers. Vendors sold everything from clothing and household utensils to toys, food, and pungent Chinese cigarettes. As always, I attracted a crowd. One man held his toddler aloft so it could get a better look at me. Two high school students took me in hand, practiced their halting English on me, bought me a sort of Chinese Popsicle, and delivered me back to the ship by bedtime.

In the morning we came upon the first of the gorges. We rounded a bend, and before us the river narrowed dramatically as it squeezed between two peaks. The sudden compression threw the current into wild confusion. Eddies and roils the size of city blocks caused the big ship to roll from side to side. The river sometimes flows at a rate of 17 miles an hour in the gorges, and can rise or fall as much as 175 feet, depending on the season and the rainfall. The gorge walls tower as high as 4,000 feet above the river surface.

A 19th-century English traveler, Isabella Bird Bishop, journeyed down the Yangtze and described her ship's terrific speed: "We went down like a flash—down smooth hills of water, where rapids had been obliterated; down leaping races, where they had been created; past hideous whirlpools, where to have been sucked in would have been destruction; past temples, pagodas, and grey cities on heights; past villages gleaming white midst dense greenery; past hill, valley, woodland, garden cultivation, and signs of industry and prosperity; past junks laid up for the summer in quiet reaches, and junks with frantic crews, straining at the sweeps, chanting wildly, bound downwards like ourselves; and still for days the Great River hurried us remorselessly along."

The mountains seemed to rise right from the water's edge. I had to crane my neck to see the tops. Every shade of green appeared on the slopes, where terraces bolstered by brick retaining walls stairstepped upward. Trails switchbacked toward passes beyond the peaks. Little stone bridges crossed ravines, and trails followed the course of the river. Tiny houses perched precariously halfway up steep slopes, where goats grazed.

A loudspeaker played taped music practically nonstop, most of it

Chinese, but I did recognize "Lady of Spain," "Danny Boy," "Red River Valley," and the refrain "You picked a fine time to leave me, Lucille."

Winds blew fiercely through the gorges that afternoon. From one of the lower decks a pack of cards escaped from someone and fluttered aft like a flock of small pink birds. It rained that evening; we sat in our cozy lounge playing backgammon as water dripped down the dark windows.

I was awakened in the night by bells ringing, whistles blowing, and lights flashing past my cabin windows. I wrapped a blanket around myself and went out on deck to see what was going on. We were docking at a waterfront ablaze with lights and bustling with activity. Crewmen tossed lines ashore as the captain nudged the big ship against the wharf. Chinese passengers hurried down the narrow gangplank, most of them carrying parcels or manhandling bicycles. Workers formed a human chain and began passing dozens of new bamboo chairs out of the hold and onto the dock. More workers carried them into a warehouse, where rats flitted in and out of the shadows. As a gentle rain began to fall, I returned, shivering, to my warm bed.

From China I journeyed to India, where another mighty river—the Ganges—creates in its final reaches a wonder that is almost too big to see. Divided between India and Bangladesh, the delta of the Ganges sprawls 250 miles from north to south and 200 miles from west to east.

The delta begins forming north of Calcutta where the Bhagirathi-Hooghly river system bears southwest from the Ganges. The Ganges carries some 900,000 tons of sediment a day into the delta, so the region is constantly building and expanding. The river meanders for miles across an immense floodplain, sloping downward to the sea at the rate of only about five inches a mile.

In recent centuries the mouth has shifted from west to east, leaving in the west a desolate area of stagnant streams and soil starved of replenishing deposits of rich silt. Forests and mangrove swamps edge the sea. The rich land of the eastern delta supports an enormous population of farmers growing wheat, millet, and barley. Rice fields flourish where rainfall is adequate.

Hindus believe that the Ganges is a goddess, Ganga, and for them the river is sacred. In Calcutta I watched thousands of devout Indians descend the long flights of steps called ghats to perform their ritual bathing in the Hooghly.

It was the time of the monsoon, and at night lightning flickered in the black sky. During the day, when the skies cleared and the sun beat down on the steaming city, air conditioners were switched to high, and in the resulting surge the lights would go out all over the city.

The port of Calcutta is one of the busiest in the Orient, and the stretch of the Hooghly between Calcutta and the sea is one of the trickiest to navigate. The Portuguese began a pilot service in 1661, but the river nonetheless is a graveyard of sunken ships; buoys and lights mark dozens of submerged hulks.

From Calcutta, follow the Ganges northward for 1,500 miles, and you will come to its remote and sacred source deep in a mountain range whose name seems a synonym for superlative—Himalaya. This is a Sanskrit word meaning "abode of snow."

The Himalayan range contains 11 of the world's 17 mountains that exceed 26,000 feet. It stretches in a mighty arc 1,600 miles from Pakistan eastward across northern India, southern Tibet, Nepal, and Bhutan. The mountains began rising some 40 million years ago during the

"mountains born of fire"

Overleaf: *Smoldering Krakatau vents sulfurous steam. On August 27, 1883, the Indonesian island—uninhabited and then much larger—blew itself up in "the greatest natural explosion in history," heard 2,200 miles away in Australia. A witness 200 miles away called the sound "simply deafening." Clouds of debris spread around the world, blocking sunlight and perhaps cooling the atmosphere for a time. Seismic sea waves killed at least 36,000 people. Today only a remnant of the island rises from the tropical waters off Java.*

GEORG GERSTER

Tertiary period, when the great Indian subcontinent, adrift on its crustal plate, began colliding with the Asian landmass.

Nearly hidden in the depths of the Himalayas is the Vale of Kashmir, another name that elicits a shiver of response, conjuring up visions of an exotic realm on the other side of the world.

It's an exquisitely green valley just 84 miles long and 25 miles wide, rimmed by snowy mountains. Kashmir's capital, Srinagar, a bustling center of commerce and tourism, hugs the shores of Dal Lake in the heart of the Vale, about 5,000 feet above sea level.

The Vale has been called "a jewel set in the heart of a rock," and its verdant beauty and temperate climate have long attracted visitors. The Mogul Emperor Jehangir called Kashmir "the paradise of which priests have prophesied and poets have sung." The British, during their long history in India, made Kashmir a popular summer retreat, and they created a feature of the place that has endured to this day. Prohibited by law from owning land here, they lived aboard luxurious houseboats moored in Dal Lake. Today some 900 houseboats, ranging from elaborate palaces to leaky shanties, line the shores of the lake. Many are available for rent by visitors. I stayed on one that boasted colorful Kashmiri carpets and hand-carved woodwork of aromatic Himalayan cedar.

Shikaras—little gondola-like boats with rakishly tilted awnings—turned the lake into a floating bazaar. Boatmen arrived at my stoop selling food, jewelry, cigarettes, flowers, furs, saffron, carpets, and shawls. One vendor had a large wooden chest filled with homemade candy. Another paddled up and asked: "You feel like silver jewels?"

One balmy morning I toured the lake with Jeff Campbell, a knowledgeable amateur naturalist who works for one of the Himalayan outfitters. Jeff is a third-generation Indian; his grandparents came from the United States as missionaries around the turn of the century.

"Where loveliness dwells and an enchantment steals over the senses,'' said India's Jawaharlal Nehru of the Vale of Kashmir. Shimmering Dal Lake reflects Himalayan peaks that guard the mile-high valley. Mogul emperors built palaces and gardens here, and the British in colonial India escaped the summer heat of the coasts and plains aboard luxurious houseboats that still welcome visitors. Flower sellers (below) and other vendors paddle sleek shikaras around the lake, hawking wares of every sort.

I felt like a prince as I reclined on the cushions of my shikara and let the boatman do all the work. He was a tall young Kashmiri named Abdul with, oddly, red hair—"a legacy," according to Jeff, "of Alexander the Great. Maybe." Or, more likely, of Aryan invaders.

Out on the water, men standing in flat-bottomed boats dredged muck from the lake bed. "They take it home and pile it up to make dikes," Jeff said. "Then they plant willows on it, and before long they've got a slightly larger piece of property."

We saw little blue kingfishers perching on willow branches, or plunging into the lake after schools of minnows that flashed in the shallows. Large black hawk-like birds called kites soared overhead.

We followed the Jhelum River through the center of Srinagar, past housewives doing their laundry, slapping clothes against rocks at the water's edge and waving as we floated by. We passed under a solid bridge built centuries ago during the days of the Mogul Empire in India, and alongside three-story brick structures also put up by the Moguls. Wooden balconies at the windows were the same brown color as the bricks.

Roses, marigolds, and crape myrtle bloomed on the banks, and women knelt in shikaras as they gathered lotus stalks. Another boat was full of drying reeds, destined to be woven into mats. Toddlers alone in shikaras did professional J-strokes to send their boats in straight lines across the lake. Ducks quacked at one another in annoyance.

Around the western end of the lake where springs bubbled from the mountainsides, Mogul emperors had built luxurious gardens. Jeff and I strolled through several of them. Terraces stairstepped down the mountains, and channels of water splashed over ledges and powered fountains

"a jewel set in the heart of a rock'"

89

that spread a cooling mist. Marigolds, zinnias, sunflowers, and roses bloomed alongside them; graceful *chinar* trees shaded the walkways.

"The gardens had fallen into disrepair over the centuries," said Jeff. "The British were largely responsible for restoring them."

That night, as I sat on a cushioned bench on the porch of my houseboat, watching fireworks light the sky across the lake, a little bird flew out of the darkness and, with a frantic flutter, came to rest on the railing at my elbow. As if in greeting, it wagged its tail—a wagtail. Apparently something had frightened it from its perch, and it had flown to the light of my boat. It hopped down onto the cushion beside me and turned to face the lake. Together we watched the fireworks.

The next morning Jeff and I set out on a two-day drive from Srinagar across the main Himalayan chain to Leh, in Ladakh, one of the most remote places in the world.

In the Vale of Kashmir, we had driven through forests of horse chestnut, pine, spruce, birch, and elderberry bushes, but when we crossed Zoji La, a pass near Kargil, and entered Ladakh, the trees and bushes disappeared. Ladakh is in a rain shadow, an arid area where only about three inches of rain fall in a year. Dusty nomads herded cattle and horses along the road.

From Leh, on the banks of the Indus River, Jeff and I went on an eight-day pony trek through the rugged countryside of Ladakh. Two Ladakhi porters and two Tibetan horsemen were along to take care of the cooking and camping chores and the packing and tending of the four little horses. We would cross a couple of passes, then ascend for two days up the Markha Valley, and finally cross a high pass above the Plains of Nimaling, before returning to Leh.

A little valley lush with irrigated barley fields led us upward out of Leh. Women singing a simple harvest song were gathering the ripe grain. We paused while Jeff chatted with them, and I learned a Ladakhi word that I would use frequently during the next few days: *joolay*, hello.

Soon we had climbed into a world of bare brown ridges and gravelly valleys, a moonscape where grouse clucked and chattered in the rocks along the trail. The hills were full of Buddhist shrines: *gompas*, little stone lamaseries or temples; *chortens*, pagodalike structures that resembled chessmen and contained religious writings; *manis*, piles of stones with prayers carved on them. Most of the stones bore the Sanskrit words "*Om Mani Padme Hum,*" "Hail to the Jewel in the Lotus," a prayer addressed to Avalokitesvara, the Buddhist god of mercy. Prayer flags fluttered atop all these structures.

We trekked beside crashing streams whose banks were lined with willow trees. Rosefinches, sparrows, and magpies flitted among the branches. Ingeniously complex irrigation channels carried water high up the valley walls.

Farmers harvesting their fields of barley stopped their singing to wave as we passed by. Ladakhi children in ragged sweaters and wool caps came up to us, grinned shyly, and asked for *bonbons*, sweets.

The thin air became thinner. Snowcapped peaks floated on the horizon, and high fluffy clouds drifted overhead. In one village, a small brick building held a huge prayer wheel: a cylinder the size and shape of a section of culvert, standing on end, with an axle running down through its center. A small arm extended outward from the top of the cylinder. With every revolution of the wheel, the arm struck the clapper of a little bell. "Each time the bell rings, a prayer flies up to heaven," said Jeff, giving the wheel a spin. We counted 25 strong clangs and one feeble one.

"a synonym for superlative -- Himalaya"

Providing for survival, climber Robert Schaller checks oxygen cylinders cached for the final push to the summit of K2 in the Karakoram Range. Assisting the 1975 United States expedition, heavy-laden porters file toward the 28,250-foot peak. Though second to Everest in height, K2 poses greater challenges to climbers, earning it the epithet "savage mountain."

Preceding pages: Regarded by the Sherpas of Nepal as the "Goddess Mother of the World," 29,028-foot Mount Everest glows in the setting sun.

93

At night when we camped, weary and footsore from a day of walking, the ponies would stand with their noses in feed bags, pawing the ground as they ate. Later, as moonglow filled my tent, I could hear the bells around their necks ringing as they grazed. Another night, one of the Tibetan horsemen smashed open the skull of a sheep with a rock so that he could cook and eat the brains. Later, I heard him chanting in the dark as he performed his Buddhist rituals. I felt a long way from home.

We crossed a pass and descended through a magnificent gorge with steep bare walls, its floor a jumble of fallen boulders. In a clump of streamside willows we stopped for lunch, and two Ladakhi girls giggled shyly nearby as we ate.

At the village of Markha we climbed to the lamasery, guided by the steady booming of a drum. Prayer flags on the roof fluttered in the breeze. We tiptoed into the cool darkness, and through a low doorway we could see a young lama, with shaven head and rust-colored robe, kneeling at his prayers. We hesitated, but he smiled and motioned us in. He continued his prayers, singing, thumping a drum, clashing a pair of cymbals. Demon masks, flags, and tapestries hung on the walls, and statues of Buddha watched from the shadows, little votive butter lamps burning before them.

We stayed only a short while at the lamasery. As we continued our climb, we saw griffon vultures and golden eagles soaring on warm thermals. Crowlike birds called choughs—pronounced chuffs—wheeled in flocks against the valley walls. We watched a group of them swoop down on a young eagle cowering on a ledge.

We met a Ladakhi girl herding a little gray donkey loaded with brushy firewood. With dainty, ladylike steps it picked its way down the steep trail, watching anxiously where it was going. As we ascended the valley, we occasionally forded the rushing stream, cold and gray from glacial silt. We'd take off our boots, and the water felt good on our hot, dusty feet. Hill pigeons fluttered along the stream, and snow leopard tracks, fairly fresh in the mud, led upward into the rocks.

Higher and higher we climbed, and I felt sometimes that it was not so much that the landscape was growing bigger, but rather that I was shrinking, becoming smaller and smaller as the enormous mountains swallowed us up. I began to imagine myself a mote in the Himalayan breeze, being wafted toward heaven like a Ladakhi prayer.

We came at last to the broad bowl of the Plains of Nimaling, just below our final pass. I was a little giddy in the thin air, and when a Tibetan hare hopped across a rocky meadow, I felt the mountains tilt. A huge, vulturelike lammergeier with a nine-foot wingspan glided over our campsite, perfectly motionless as it peered down past its beard at us.

Next morning there was frost on our tents, ice in our water bucket.

As we began our final climb, I picked up a little piece of granite to carry along. Each stone added to the cairns at the passes represents another prayer, Jeff had said. At the pass, at 17,300 feet, the sharp wind had ripped the prayer flags to tatters. A bumblebee too cold to fly was turning somersaults in the shadow of a prayer wall. I flicked it into the sunshine and watched as the warmth revived it. Feeling a trifle self-conscious, I added my little rock to the pile on a prayer wall and, with the bells of Asia ringing in my memory, hoped for the best for our world and all the wonders in it.

"Snowcapped peaks floated on the horizon"

Guarded by the eternal Himalayas, the lamasery of Tikse rises on a knoll in Ladakh, India's remotest district. A Tibetan form of Buddhism permeates the Ladakhi culture. At lamaseries and shrines throughout this mountain kingdom, clanging prayer wheels and chanting voices fill the air in tribute to Buddha. Here, as in other parts of Asia, the sacred becomes inseparable from the natural wonder.

LYNN ABERCROMBIE

Australia
and the Pacific Islands

By Cynthia Russ Ramsay
Photographs by
David Austen

T he vast expanse of the Pacific, largest ocean on earth, holds mountains higher than Everest and canyons deeper than any on land. In that awesome vastness, far greater in area than all the continents combined, one could spend a lifetime of exploration. Poring over maps and talking with scientists, I planned a journey that would let me sample the natural marvels of Australia and a few of the 20,000 islands in that boundless sea.

There was, however, one voyage of slightly less than seven miles that I could not make. But then, only once has anyone been to the bottom of the world—to the Challenger Deep. About 220 miles south of Guam, the Mariana Trench, the 1,835-mile-long submarine canyon in the floor of the Pacific, plunges to 35,810 feet, the greatest known depth in all the oceans.

On January 23, 1960, the bathyscaph *Trieste*, a sphere with steel walls 4¾ inches thick and equipped with powerful floodlights, descended into the unending darkness and eternal cold of the abyss. After four hours and 43 minutes, *Trieste* settled on a flat surface of ivory-colored sediment, and through the thick plastic portholes Swiss engineer Jacques Piccard and American oceanographer Lt. Don Walsh, USN, looked out upon a world never seen before.

They were astonished to see, in the glare of the floodlights, a sole-like fish and a "beautiful" red shrimp, but the ocean floor was essentially a featureless plain with neither animal tracks nor mounds nor burrows—only "some minor undulations suggestive of animal plowings."

I did not make the trip into the Challenger Deep, did not see its "crystal clear" waters that had "not the slightest trace of plankton," never encountered what Piccard described as "a vast emptiness beyond all comprehension." But my itinerary across the Pacific—to Hawaii, Bora Bora, Australia, and New Zealand—led me to landscapes equally remarkable, each in its own way.

There is, for example, nothing quite like the volcanoes on the island of Hawaii. One of them, Mauna Loa, is the largest mountain in the world. This single active volcano has a mass greater than the entire Sierra Nevada range in California. Its enormous bulk, formed of molten rock oozing and exploding from a rupture in the earth's crust, gradually ascends from the ocean floor to the gigantic height of 31,907 feet. Neighboring Mauna Kea, dormant now, is even higher. From a depth of 18,240 feet its gentle slopes and rounded dome soar another 13,796 feet above the sea. Measured from the ocean floor, these two volcanoes are the highest mountains on earth.

Both peaks, scientists now believe, were born of the same source of magma—a hot spot far below the planet's crust that has been producing

Stark as a moonscape, the pitted surface of Ayers Rock spreads beneath the desert sky in the heart of the Australian outback. Aboriginal tribes revere the sandstone monolith, tracing its origin to the beginning of the world.

Overleaf: Snow-dusted summit of Mauna Kea— "white mountain"— towers 13,796 feet above the tropical island of Hawaii. Cinder cones dot the slopes of the long-dormant volcano.

GORDON W. GAHAN (OVERLEAF)

volcanoes for at least 70 million years. As the Pacific crustal plate has drifted northwest more than 30 feet a century over this stationary furnace, a steady succession of volcanoes and volcanic islands has appeared. Of the islands that make up the Hawaiian archipelago, Hawaii at the southeastern end is geologically the youngest, and Kilauea, the restless mountain in the southeast corner of that island, ranks among the most active volcanoes anywhere.

Beneath the low, heavy clouds that hid the summits of Mauna Loa and Mauna Kea, I stood on the rim of Kilauea's caldera, nearly ten miles in circumference. I looked down on a lifeless landscape of lava that had congealed into dark, crumpled rock. In the sepulchral stillness 400 feet below, nothing moved. Only plumes of steam, produced as groundwater seeped into some buried inferno of molten rock, drifted a little distance before disappearing into the chill, gray mist.

The rock underfoot was unstable in places as I walked down into the caldera with Brian Goring, a ranger at the Hawaii Volcanoes National Park. We picked our way over a patchwork of lava, which had hardened into brittle crusts that might collapse onto the layer below. More often the lava had spread like taffy and cooled into solid slabs. The massive flows had solidified into motionless rivers. Lava that had continued to move as it began to congeal formed a jumble of angular clumps.

Greatest of the oceans, the Pacific covers 65 million square miles—nearly one-third of the world's surface. Beneath its waters lies the lowest point on earth, the Challenger Deep in the Mariana Trench. Measured from the ocean floor, Mauna Kea in Hawaii is the world's tallest mountain. Other wonders of the Pacific and its more than 20,000 islands include Australia's Great Barrier Reef, New Zealand's fiords, and Bora Bora.

And lava that had spurted into the sky, then cooled and clotted as it fell, formed a loose debris of porous cinders.

This desolation of raw lava was the beginning. From it, the island had grown, acre by fiery acre. From rivers of incandescent rock heated to 2000°F, from fountains of fire spouting higher than the Empire State Building, from hailstorms of cinders had come the substance that in time weathered into Hawaii's fertile soil. The fields of sugarcane, the wooded valleys with their orchids and anthuriums, the green grazing lands, and the orchards of coffee, papaya, and macadamia trees all owe their existence to the volcanoes. As if these were not enough, there are scalloped beaches where white surf foams across black sand. There the hot lava had sizzled into the sea with such an explosion of steam that the rock was pulverized into fragments, which the waves polished into sand.

Hawaiian Islands

"Even though the lava has destroyed forests and farms and has threatened the city of Hilo a few times, Hawaii's volcanoes are tamer than most," said Brian, as he led me to Halemaumau, the still smoking crater within Kilauea's caldera and the main vent through which so much lava has poured. "We don't have explosions like the one at Mount St. Helens in 1980, which blasted clouds of steam, ash, and volcanic dust into the sky and blew part of the mountain away. The lavas here are very fluid, and they normally erupt before great pressures build. So we end up with volcanoes that are safer to approach."

Countless visitors have been drawn to Kilauea since 1823, when one of the first missionaries to Hawaii, William Ellis, gazed into Halemaumau and saw "one vast flood of burning matter in a state of terrific ebullition." Another visitor in the 1800s described the lava "furiously bubbling and boiling and dashing up waves of red-hot foam and spray."

For 101 years, from 1823 to 1924, Halemaumau was almost continuously active and contained a lava lake that rose and fell. More than 35 times since then lava has gushed from the crater or spurted in orange-hot jets from a series of vents along a 50-mile fracture in the mountain's flank. Lava flared to the surface along this rift zone in January 1983. Just 24 hours before plumes of molten rock lighted up the sky, seismometers at the Hawaii Volcano Observatory detected a swarm of small quakes as the magma broke through more than two miles of crust. Seismometers also picked up harmonic tremors, signals scientists correlate with the movement of magma underground. A larger eruption from this same

Bora
Bora

Tahiti

PACIFIC
OCEAN

North
Island

NEW
ZEALAND

Tasman
Sea

South
Island

SOUTHERN
ALPS

Mt. Cook
12,349 FT.

Fiordland N.P.

0   KILOMETERS   800
0   STATUTE MILES   600

fracture in 1959 engulfed a rain forest dense with ferns and crimson-flowering ohias. It left a waste of black, barren cinders and a cemetery of blanched, denuded trees.

In the persistent rain I shivered from cold—or perhaps from melancholy—as I set out along Devastation Trail, a wooden walkway built by the National Park Service across this no-man's-land. But soon I came upon a strange and wonderful thing. Slender ferns squeezed up here and there from crannies among the cinders. One little shrub after another sprouted amid the stones. Lichens etched the fallen branches with their pale green signatures. The lava was rotting. Life was blossoming. The tormented land was being reborn in a process I found heartening.

No lava scars or skeletal trees mar the green tranquillity of Bora Bora, a small tropical island 2,400 miles south of Hawaii, in French Polynesia. No eruptions threaten the crystal waters of its lagoon or the single paved road that winds along the coast under a canopy of palms. But Bora Bora, whose very name conjures visions of a South Seas paradise, is volcanic, too. It consists of a volcano—a long-extinct, eroded volcano that is slowly sinking into the sea. The craggy remnants of the crater give the island its twin peaks and its unforgettable profile.

The drowned rim of the volcano served as a platform for reef-building corals. A barrier reef encircles the island in a ring of coral and gentles the Pacific into a shallow lagoon. Parts of the reef appear above the surface as low, sun-bleached cays. The one channel through the reef faces Vaitape, the island's downtown, where men with flowers behind their ears sit in the shade and sip beer, and girls with long black hair, bright sarong-like *pareos*, and bold smiles whiz by on motorcycles.

A 50-minute plane ride from Tahiti had brought me to Bora Bora—to its sandy islets, called *motus*, and its lush mainland—a place that some have extolled as the loveliest in the world. Thousands are lured here each year, making tourism the main business for the 2,500 inhabitants. A few who came have been so beguiled by the natural beauty, the balmy climate, and the amiable Polynesians that they have stayed on.

"Why do I choose to live here?" Colette Victor, a green-eyed Parisian elegant in a pareo, echoed my question. "At 40 or so, you realize you can't have everything in life. You have to seize the essentials, and they are very small things: the sun warm on my skin, soft sand beneath my bare feet, the lagoon sparkling at my doorstep, fresh flowers for my hair, and especially the time to enjoy my family. I feel good here."

Colette's husband, Paul Emile, is a noted polar explorer. When the Victors bought their motu 25 years ago, they found the fair skies, the gentle trade winds, and the marvelous views of their dreams. But beneath the palms their land was a tangle of brush accommodating squadrons of mosquitoes. Now only white doves flutter to the rafters of their A-frame house, which has one side open to plantings of hibiscus and bougainvillea, a sliver of beach, and the luminous sea.

"My only regret is that we did not come sooner."

No such decision was necessary for Poro Tama, a lean, taciturn man with a swift smile. Poro has always lived on Bora Bora. A descendant of brown-skinned warriors who paddled swift canoes to raid the neighboring islands, he relies on an outboard motor to reach his fish traps in the lagoon. Poro likes to get an early start so that he can sell his catch by 9 a.m.

"I'll pick you up at six," said Poro's partner, Keith Olson, a 34-year-old suntanned American who came to French Polynesia 15 years ago.

Silvery waterfalls vein the cliffs of Waimanu Valley on the island of Hawaii. The Hawaiian Islands (above), summits of an oceanic ridge, began forming more than 25 million years ago, when molten rock started spurting from a fissure in the seafloor.

Overleaf: Fluffy clouds obscure the twin peaks of Bora Bora in French Polynesia. A barrier reef formed of coral encircles the island and its lagoon.

N.G.S. PHOTOGRAPHER GEORGE F. MOBLEY; GORDON W. GAHAN (OVERLEAF)

A few land crabs were scuttling across the road as we drove into Poro's hibiscus-hedged yard. Chickens tottered out of the way, toward the rounded hulks of two black pigs. Red, orange, and purple pareos were drying on a line beside some mango, banana, and breadfruit trees.

After a hasty breakfast, we set out in Poro's weathered skiff toward the outer reef. The lagoon was a dazzle of colors shimmering like silk in the sunlight. Pale green in the shallows, the water turned to aqua and azure and sapphire farther out. In the distance, beyond the white line of surf where the Pacific meets the reef and wave upon wave explodes into spray, the ocean gleamed a deep indigo.

I watched a leopard ray flutter along in the shallows, its implausible disk shape clearly visible in the transparent sea. As we chugged along, I could pick out colonies of spiny sea urchins, and nestled in the sandy bottom were huge *Tridacna* clams, their shells agape, exposing mantles like lips of turquoise velvet.

We stopped beside a series of stakes driven into the lagoon floor. The stakes supported chicken-wire fences that had funneled bass, snappers, spotted groupers, and squirrel fish into a large, circular wire trap. With mask and snorkel, Keith jumped into the water, netting and spearing the day's catch. After two more stops, Poro was ready to return, sell his fish, and take the rest of the day off.

All too soon, I had to board another boat, the launch that carries passengers to the airport, which is built on a cay. As I crossed the lagoon, all the scenes I had come to love were in view, for like Bali-ha'i, the enchanted isle in James Michener's *Tales of the South Pacific*, Bora Bora is small: "Like a jewel, it could be perceived in one loving glance."

From the small dimensions and easily accessible beauty of Bora Bora, my journey took me to the immense undersea world of Australia's Great Barrier Reef—home of the most diverse fauna anywhere. Filled with strange and still unfathomed wonders, it is the longest reef on earth, extending 1,250 miles along Australia's northeast coast.

The Great Barrier Reef is not a single continuous structure. It is a labyrinth of more than 2,000 reefs—not all of them charted, not all of them explored—and several hundred islands and cays, some of only an acre or two and built of coral sand.

Millions of years ago, according to marine biologists, native corals evolved in these waters, settling in the clear, warm, shallow seas. Corals begin life as free-swimming microscopic larvae. When one finds a firm surface, it permanently attaches itself and becomes a mature polyp. Each polyp secretes a limestone cup, a skeleton for its soft, tiny body.

Some polyps are male; some are female; and some polyps can be both or neither. It doesn't matter that much, because they all have another way of reproducing: A new polyp will bud off from its parent and secrete its skeleton on the limestone of the previous generation.

As the polyps of the Great Barrier Reef reproduced themselves ceaselessly in colonies, they created a stony landscape of headlands and pinnacles, canyons and grottoes. Only the top or outer layer is formed of living coral, which at first sight produces disbelief—and then wonder.

More than 350 species of coral have constructed thickets of slender branches, rounded boulders furrowed and convoluted like the human brain, and plates scalloped like the leaves of water lilies. There are clusters of petals, clumps of pompons, whorls of knobby fingers, and rows of graceful fans, all ranging in color from the palest blue and lavender to saffron yellow and rose. (Continued on page 112)

"a profusion and variety found nowhere else"

Shimmering wave of damselfish sweeps past scuba divers on the Great Barrier Reef, haven for thousands of marine animal species. Stretching more than 1,200 miles, the chain of coral reefs, islands, and cays breaks the force of Pacific waters (above) along Australia's northeast coast.

107

A thousand feet above the desert floor, climbers explore the furrowed summit of Ayers Rock. The massive formation and the Olgas in the distance survive as remnants of an eroded mountain range. Paintings on cave walls in the rock's base depict subjects sacred to the Aboriginals—Australia's earliest inhabitants. Today Ayers Rock casts its spell over tourists (opposite), who watch the play of late afternoon sunlight on ancient sandstone.

Following pages: Back from a rabbit hunt, tribeswomen rest around a brush fire at day's end. Some Aboriginals, preferring the old ways, still manage to wrest a living from the harsh outback.

This extravagance of shape and color provides shelter and a measure of security for a population of creatures living together in a profusion and variety found nowhere else. Sponges, starfish, and sea slugs in vivid hues; feather stars that cast off their arms when in danger; dainty cone shells inhabited by creatures whose sting can kill a man; clams that

Called Aorangi—"cloud piercer"—by the Maoris, Mount Cook, in the Southern Alps, thrusts its snowy summit to an elevation of 12,349 feet. Climbers on a nearby ridge gain an unimpeded view of the peak, highest in New Zealand. The wind-whipped slopes of the Southern Alps offer climbing challenges equal to any in the world. Sir Edmund Hillary, a New Zealander, brought his team here to train before their successful assault on Mount Everest in 1953.

can weigh more than 500 pounds; worms with bristles, worms that look like feather dusters, and worms resembling lengths of bright ribbon; and species of fishes that can change sex and color.

"And we're still finding creatures man has never seen before," said Dr. Walter A. Starck, an American marine biologist now living in Australia. "On one dive, for example, I collected a bag of sand from the seafloor next to a reef for a colleague at the Australian Museum. In that one bag were more than 300 species of micromollusks—snails and bivalves—most of them completely new to science.

"It is time that has made the coral reef such a prodigal place. The Great Barrier Reef has existed as a continuous definable community for 20 million years, so evolution has been able to proceed there in a great many specializing ways.

"One of the things we find is an incredible range of defenses. Some animals manufacture highly toxic poisons; some produce electric shocks; some have armor or spines. Some defenses are on a cellular level. On the reef, animals live in a soup of waste products of every creature, so they have developed defenses against infection. Medical researchers are now looking at the active biochemical compounds in the cells of reef animals as promising sources of medicines.

"Another characteristic of the crowded reef is the extraordinary color patterns of the fishes. Scientists have logged more than 1,400 species of fishes there, and with so many animals living together, the stripes, the spots, the gaudy splotches of color may be badges of identity. In other cases the colors may serve as camouflage."

At Cairns, a charming tropical town in northern Queensland, I boarded *Reef Explorer*, a 60-foot diving vessel, whose 12 passengers included a number of snorkelers like me. After motoring due east about four hours, we came to the lighthouse marking Grafton Passage, one of the main shipping channels, and found ourselves in the gloriously transparent waters of the outer reef.

I slid off the sea-level platform at the stern and slipped into water neither warm nor cold, but with the sensuous feel of silk. A school of small, iridescent fish streaked by in a silvery shimmer. Elongated cornet fish hung motionless in disarray like a heap of jackstraws, then sped away in an instant V-formation as I swam near. Black-and-white Moorish idols cruised along with their dorsal fins elongated into filaments that trailed elegantly behind them. Vermilion coral cod with pale blue dots, green and purple wrasses, blue and yellow surgeon fish with scalpel-sharp barbs at the base of their tails paraded through the sunlit waters. The scarlet fronds of a feather star undulated on a yellow lobe of soft coral.

A pair of butterfly fish, their colorful bodies so flat they seemed two-dimensional, darted to and fro, patrolling a patch of blue staghorn coral that was their territory. Dozens of parrot fish, pink and yellow or blue and green, pecked at the coral, snapping off bits with their fused, beaklike front teeth and feeding on the polyps inside. A small soldierfish disappeared into a cranny of purple coral. And scores and scores of fishes whose names I never learned, but whose beauty I will always remember, appeared and then disappeared into the dim blue distance.

Although this fantastic world enthralled me, I was never totally at ease. The unblinking stare of the fishes unnerved me. And there were the sharks. I never saw any except the harmless white-tipped reef shark, but they are always around. As they were the time we dined on fresh mackerel, and someone on board tossed the fish head into the water. In an instant two sharks materialized.

"In my surveys, I've seen hundreds of sharks, but only once was I worried," said Dr. John Veron, a marine biologist engaged in sorting and reclassifying all the reef-building corals of eastern Australia.

"When a shark circles very fast and makes sudden turns, chances are it will attack. And when it does, its speed is unbelievable," Dr. Veron told me as we talked in his office at the Australian Institute of Marine Sciences in Townsville, Queensland. In his one confrontation with a shark, he warded off an attack by wielding a chunk of coral as a club.

Sharks are not the only predators in the fish-eat-fish world of the coral reef, but aggression among corals surprised me.

"Corals continuously fight with each other for space by threatening to overgrow their neighbors," Dr. Veron explained, "and many species retaliate by growing long sweeper tentacles with powerful stinger cells. These tentacles take a week or two to grow, but the neighboring coral isn't closing in all that fast. As these tentacles touch the target, they adhere and after a while kill the encroaching coral.

"Some species can also produce filaments that actually digest the tissues of other corals, and soft corals leak poison into the water, which can destroy any coral that comes too close.

"Coral only about as large as a fist may control an area several times its size. Scientists have long wondered why 10 to 50 percent of the limestone surface of a reef is unoccupied by living coral. I think we have at least one of the answers now."

A complex relationship exists between corals and the one-celled algae called zooxanthellae, which live in the soft tissues of polyps.

"Reef-building corals couldn't survive without them," said Dr. Edward Drew, another scientist on the marine institute's staff. "The polyps use the oxygen and carbohydrates the zooxanthellae produce, while the algae take up and recycle the coral's metabolic *(Continued on page 118)*

"endless vistas of soaring, snowy peaks and pinnacled ridges"

Overleaf: Gleaming snows of Mount Cook, right center, and sister peaks give way to evergreen forests sweeping down to the sea. Capt. James Cook, who reached New Zealand's South Island in 1770, described these mountains as "prodigious" in height and "cover'd in many places with large patches of snow which perhaps have laid their sence the creation."

GORDON W. GAHAN

Sunlight dapples the moss-draped Milford Track—''finest walk in the world'' for many seasoned hikers. The 33-mile trail winds through rain forest and mountain wilderness in Fiordland National Park. Streams lace this lush corner of New Zealand; waterfalls drench slopes carpeted with ferns, lichens, and alpine flowers.

wastes. And by some process we still don't fully understand, the algae induce the corals to grow and calcify. Actually the zooxanthellae have as much a role in producing limestone as the coral polyps themselves."

From scientists like Ed Drew, I had learned that the Great Barrier Reef was not only a marvelously colorful, beautiful realm, but also an astonishingly intricate, infinitely varied one.

Life is much less prolific in the outback, the harsh interior of Australia. In the dusty heart of the outback, where desert oaks and stunted mulga trees provide occasional shade, the solitary mass of Ayers Rock dramatically interrupts the monotony of red sand and prickly spinifex grasses.

Arriving at Ayers Rock on a short flight from Alice Springs, I first saw the rounded hump of sandstone, with its sheer, undulating walls and flattened top, from the air. A stark, enigmatic survivor of long-vanished mountains, Ayers Rock has an impact, an effect on the emotions, beyond that of its immense size and great age. It rises 1,143 feet above the surrounding desert, and covers 1,200 acres; its origin lies 500 million years in the past, when sand was deposited here in an inland sea. This sediment became sandstone, which was uplifted into a mountain range and then worn down to a flat plain. But Ayers Rock endured.

Statistics and geologic facts cannot convey the massive dignity of the place. It seems to smolder with a mysterious energy, an illusion that comes, perhaps, from its changing colors. It picks up the rose of dawn; at midday, when the sun beats down and heat radiates from the rock, it glows like a giant orange ember; and sunset kindles it into a blood-red fire that cools to lavender at twilight.

Aboriginals once roamed this region, stalking kangaroos, wallabies, and emus and gathering figs and grass seeds. For them, the springs at Ayers Rock assured a water supply in the long season of drought. The caves at the base of the rock gave shelter in the shorter season of rains. Ayers Rock, or Uluru as the Aboriginals call it, was long a ceremonial center for the Yankuntjatjara and Pitjantjatara tribes.

"To understand the significance of Ayers Rock to the Aboriginals, you have to understand their intimate relationship with the land," said Derek Roff, chief ranger in charge of Uluru National Park since 1968.

Over the years Derek has won the confidence of the Ayers Rock Aboriginals. "But," he will hasten to say, "there's a great deal that has not been revealed to me, and questioning the Aboriginals before they are ready to tell you will only bring the wrong answers."

Talking with Derek as we walked around the rock in the stifling heat of afternoon, I learned something about the Aboriginals' ties to their tribal land. The Aboriginals believe that their ancestors, part human and part animal, created the landscape as they traveled across the countryside during Dreamtime, when the world began. An ancestor's campfire became a rock hole; the place where an ancestor had bled in battle became a watercourse. All the deeds and events are chronicled in myths that form the sacred lore of the tribe. These stories of Dreamtime, passed on for untold generations, are a major force in the Aboriginals' life, and give them a special kinship with the land.

"The Aboriginals dazzle me with their knowledge of the land," said Derek. "They seem to know every blade of grass. Imagine, an old man can recognize the spot in the sandhills where his people killed a kangaroo when he was a boy!"

My sojourn at Ayers Rock gave me only a brief glimpse into the spirit-filled world of the Australian Aboriginal. My excursion into the wild, precipitous mountains of New Zealand's Southern Alps gave me endless vistas of soaring, snowy peaks and pinnacled ridges, lovely shapes that would vanish in snow or sleet or mist within an hour or two. In the catalog of earth's mountain ranges, the Southern Alps are nowhere near the loftiest, but few are so steep or so formidable. These are, after all, the mountains where Sir Edmund Hillary trained for his conquest of Everest in 1953.

"Few places in the world have such vicious, variable weather," said professional alpine guide Shaun Norman, who leads expeditions into the high country of Mount Cook National Park.

"What makes these mountains different and dangerous is their proximity to the sea. In a scant 16 miles, they rise from a lush coastal rain forest to a barrens of sandstone, snow, and ice. Winds heavy with moisture-laden air shriek in from the turbulent Tasman Sea, bringing savage storms that can strand and kill."

But Mount Cook, at 12,349 feet the highest peak in New Zealand, was basking in the sun the day I set out with Shaun. Our journey began with a flight to the small, snowbound Annette Plateau—a perch high on Mount Sealy that brought many peaks into closer view. We took off in a ski plane over the Tasman Valley. Below us, the runoff from the Tasman Glacier poured into a web of streams, gray with finely ground glacial debris. Small ponds dimpled the toe of the glacier with circles of pale jade, where the sun had melted sinkholes in the ice. Silvery rivulets trickled from snowfields down impossibly steep scree slopes and disappeared into the gravelly moraine. Ahead, the sweeping, 18-mile-long glacier itself smothered the valley of its own making, dragging fragments of the mountain in its invisible flow.

The plane banked sharply to turn up into Mueller Valley. Above its main glacier, smaller tributary ones tumbled down slopes so steep the ice fractured into the awesome chaos of an icefall, riddled with crevasses. Finally, the plane swooped to a landing on what seemed too small a spot, sliding into a turn and a timely halt in the soft snow.

Alert for hidden crevasses, Shaun led the way across a snowfield.

"Sometimes the only indication you have is a small crack in the surface of the snow. Sometimes a narrow ridge of snow is a warning. Unless you watch out for these telltale signs, you'll be right into it—a total commitment to falling."

As we descended, snow gave way to boulder fields, and before each step I wondered where to place my foot. With each small leap from boulder to boulder, my backpack bounced, and I barely maintained my balance by using an ice ax as a walking stick; my teetering progress was heralded by the sharp clink of metal against rock.

A far nobler sound was the deep rumble of avalanches thundering down adjacent slopes in great billows of powdery snow. And any time my eyes left my feet, there was the serene beauty of the mountains. I stopped to watch clouds spilling over Mount Sefton's snowy crest. The clouds curled down the leeward side only briefly before vanishing over the valley on a continuous journey into oblivion.

Before long, my equilibrium was restored as we devoured dinner in the Mueller Hut, a snug timbered shelter built astride a barren saddle and blessed with an inspiring view.

The Mount Cook region is a nascent land, and much of it remains

"The plant-choked landscape, with its lavish rains and scant sunlight"

imprisoned in ice. At the southern end of the Alps, however, in New Zealand's Fiordland National Park, nearly all the glaciers retreated 14,000 years ago, leaving behind rugged, knife-edged ridges and steep-walled, U-shaped valleys. Some valleys were so deep they were drowned by the Tasman Sea as the ice melted. Fourteen of these long, narrow arms of ocean indent 200 miles of the southwest coast, thrusting inland into primeval forests thick with beeches, mosses, and ferns. The plant-choked landscape, with its lavish rains and scant sunlight, runs from mountain heights right down to the water's edge.

In days gone by, a variety of people had come to the wooded fiord country—the native Polynesian population of Maoris, the great European navigators, the sealers and whalers, explorers, and gold seekers. Little remains of the stations where sealers and whalers caroused—and then went out to slaughter their quarry almost to extinction. The gold towns on Preservation Inlet crumbled and decayed after the ore ran out at the end of the 19th century. Even the band of Maoris that had sought refuge there from another tribe dwindled and passed away.

Except for the people who operate the tourist facilities on Milford Sound and Doubtful Sound, no one now inhabits the land. But fishermen challenge the rough, capricious waters to haul up their lobster pots.

"Bait is anything you can catch—mackerel, blue cod. It's the lobster tails that bring in the money," say the fishermen. But the lobsters grow scarce, and so the men maneuver their boats closer and closer to the rocky shores, where the catch is best and the work most dangerous.

Aboard *Shaylene*, a sleek 50-foot cutter, we would occasionally see

one of these brave little boats bobbing in the swells as it hovered close to shore. On our journey from Doubtful Sound to Dusky Sound, we were cruising along a coast as rugged and wild as it was when Capt. James Cook first found his way to the fiords in the 1770s.

*S*haylene was dwarfed by the towering, jagged scarps that hem in Doubtful Sound. I felt the impassive presence of the wilderness all around me. The sea was a black mirror whose rippling surface reflected the trackless forests. The rumble of *Shaylene*'s engine seemed jarringly out of place.

"The wind is on the nose. It's coming right down the sound, and this is too confined an area to sail into the wind," said skipper Les Hutchins, as disappointed as I that he could not unfurl the sails. Captain Cook, after all, had named the sound but had never entered here because he was "doubtful" that the winds would let his bark, the *Endeavour*, sail out.

Cook, however, did spend almost six weeks in Dusky Sound, finding "rest and sustenance" after four months in the South Pacific. We arrived at Cook's safe anchorage after pitching and yawing for hours in the four-foot swells and irregular waves of the Tasman Sea. A short walk took us to the site where Cook's astronomer had cleared trees for an observatory. The moss-smothered stumps with their adz marks stood like tombstones marking man's passage through this unspoiled, enchanted corner of New Zealand. And this enclave of primitive beauty rivaled all the other wonders I had seen on my journey across the Pacific.

"long, narrow arms of ocean... thrusting inland"

Beneath forested cliffs, a sailboat breaches the solitude of Doubtful Sound. Captain Cook's reports of seal-rich harbors lured sealing gangs to the fiords of South Island in the late 1700s. Sealers, gold seekers, and other intruders departed long ago, and Fiordland remains a nearly pristine wilderness. At right, alpine vegetation clings to Mary Peak, a promontory high above Caswell Sound.

Overleaf: Low-lying clouds enfold mountain summits in Fiordland National Park, where glaciers in ages past gouged valleys out of solid rock.

Antarctica

By Cynthia Russ Ramsay

Frozen wilderness of Antarctica engulfs a lone geologist on The Tusk, a barren marble peak jutting above the flat expanse of Liv Glacier. One of hundreds on the ice-covered continent, the glacier flows through the Transantarctic Mountains to the Ross Ice Shelf.

Overleaf: King penguins three feet tall parade on a subantarctic island. The seabirds flourish in the region's frigid waters.

So remote, so desolate, so savage a place is Antarctica that only in this century did anyone succeed in exploring it. Isolated by ferocious seas and barricaded nine months of the year by a broad belt of ice, the mainland was not even seen until early 1820. During that southern summer, ships from Russia, Great Britain, and the United States skirted the icebergs that loomed out of the mist, and men beheld the frozen continent for the first time.

But the excruciating cold, the bludgeoning winds, and the treacherous ice prevented exploration of the interior for nearly another hundred years. Not until the heroic expeditions of Norwegian explorer Roald Amundsen and Britain's Ernest Shackleton and Robert Scott did mankind penetrate the continent, larger than the United States and Mexico combined. Using sledges hauled by huskies, Amundsen's team was the first to reach the South Pole, planting the Norwegian flag there on December 14, 1911. The five men had struggled across miles of sastrugi, ice-hard ridges of snow carved by the wind. Fighting their way up steep glaciers, they had crossed the Transantarctic Mountains. Finally they had entered the high plateau, endlessly white, nearly featureless, and smothered in ice almost two miles deep at the Pole.

Much has changed since the early, historic journeys. Under the terms of the Antarctic Treaty of 1961, which dedicates the continent to peaceful purposes, about a dozen nations operate more than 30 year-round research stations in the barren emptiness of the mainland and on adjacent islands. Helicopters and planes on skis ferry scientists to bases and field camps where they study subjects ranging from penguin behavior to the effects of the ice sheet on world climate. Saunas, Jacuzzis, and a gymnasium help keep the staff in shape at McMurdo Station, the main U.S. base, where as many as 800 people work during the austral summer. Video-cassette television provides entertainment at many stations.

But much remains the same. Winter temperatures still plunge to minus 85°F and lower—in cold that makes steel brittle and destroys bare flesh in moments. Dense clouds diffuse the glare from the snow, creating dangerous whiteouts that reduce the world to a bewildering place without shadows, where distance and depth are impossible to judge.

"You can walk into a wall of snow and not see it," said Edmund Stump, a professor of geology at Arizona State University and a veteran of seven antarctic summers.

Glaciers the length of Delaware creep through the Transantarctic Mountains, and the Ross Ice Shelf covers an area of water almost as large as France. Winter brings 24-hour nights and relentless winds with velocities that reach 200 miles an hour. And the desert climate of Antarctica has not changed for the last 20 million years.

"Most of Antarctica is as dry as the Sahara. What little precipitation there is usually doesn't go anywhere. It just blows around," Ed

ARCTIC OCEAN

GREENLAND

+ *Mt. McKinley (Denali)* 20,320 FT.

Mackenzie

Great Slave Lake

Hudson Bay

PACIFIC OCEAN

R O C K Y

←*Athabasca River*

Mt. Shackleton 10,800 FT.

• Edmonton

←*Saskatchewan River*

Columbia River→

Columbia Icefield

Cascade Range

Missouri

Lake Superior

St. Lawrence

Five Islands
• St. Andrews

Montreal •

Bay of Fundy

□ Crater Lake N.P.

Billings •

□ Yellowstone N.P.

M O U N T A I N S

Boise •

Sierra Nevada

Snake

Bryce Canyon N.P. □

Arches N.P. □

Sequoia N.P. □
Death Valley N.M. □
-282 FT.

Los Angeles •

Colorado

□ Grand Canyon N.P.

• Louisville

□ Mammoth Cave N.P.

Nashville •

Mississippi

ATLANTIC OCEAN

KILOMETERS
0   1000

STATUTE MILES
0   600

□ National Park or National Monument

Chandeleur Islands

Everglades N.P. □   • Miami

Gulf of Mexico

nature. To stand on the rim and let your gaze drop slowly is to take in an expanse of rock representing almost one and a half billion years of the earth's history. More than a dozen distinct layers of sedimentary rock appear as bands on the canyon walls. To geologists, these different colored layers of sandstone, limestone, and shale—all unveiled by erosion—are records of how this place looked and what lived here over an immense period of time. The various layers tell of tropical seas, deserts with high dunes, and lowlands covered with swamps and sluggish rivers.

When I first visited the Grand Canyon several years before, I rode a wooden dory down the Colorado, hurtling through its more than 150 rapids. The first person to lead a recorded expedition down this tumultuous river was John Wesley Powell, a one-armed former Civil War officer who later headed the U. S. Geological Survey. Setting off in 1869 with four boats and nine men, Powell encountered risk and hardship nearly every day in the Grand Canyon as he battled his way down the "Great Unknown" with its "mad white foam." Now as many as 18,000 people run the Colorado rapids each year.

Instead of journeying by river, which can take anywhere from one to three weeks on the various tours, you can descend through time in the Grand Canyon simply by hiking from rim to river, which the hardiest among us can do in half a day. One morning in May, I joined seven other backpackers at Monument Point on the north rim for a week's walk into the canyon. As we maneuvered along the switchbacks, we often reached out and touched the rock as if it were Braille and on it we could read some of the earth's history. We ran our fingers over fossilized shell fragments of a clamlike invertebrate called a brachiopod, embedded in limestone that formed in a warm sea 250 million years ago. We traced on shale the labyrinthine paths of worms that had inched through mud 500 million years ago, when life was emerging from the seas.

We took two days to reach the desert-like floor of the canyon. As we approached the Colorado River, we hiked on a ledge above a narrow side canyon whose gleaming walls twisted and turned. Where the small canyon ended, a tall cascade—Deer Creek Falls—poured down a cliff, leading us to the river. Here we gazed upon rock 1.7 billion years old— the Vishnu Schist. Black and jagged, the rock jutted out of the water at a sharp angle. We struggled to comprehend its age, and the staggering fact that the schist formed the roots of an eroded mountain range that once was as high as the Himalayas. Like John Wesley Powell, we had come to "the depths of the earth . . . and we but pigmies, running up and down the sands or lost among the boulders."

Leaving the depths of the Grand Canyon, I traveled to a still lower place, on the floor of Death Valley, lowest point in the Western Hemisphere. Early one spring morning, I took a solo hike to find the exact point. It was marked on my topographical map with an "X," and the information, "282 feet below sea level." I started at minus 260 feet.

I didn't need a guidebook to remind me that Death Valley, a 140-mile-long desert basin in southeastern California, is the hottest and driest place in North America. Seeing the sun-scorched wasteland and feeling the sweat pour from my body, I easily recalled this fact. Summer temperatures here regularly rise to 120°F. The record temperature of 134° in 1913—taken in the shade—falls short by only two degrees of the world mark set in the Libyan desert in 1922. Rainfall averages one and a half inches a year. The forecast for the day of my hike read "Fair. High expected, 105°F. Winds 10 to 15 mph, with gusts up to 50 mph."

My feet crunched over blisterlike mounds of salt and silt. A cooling thought presented itself: Some 20,000 years ago, a lake 600 feet deep had covered the floor of Death Valley. I was now walking across the ancient lake bed. A much shallower lake occupied the valley floor 2,000 years ago. The climate changed and the lake evaporated, leaving behind, like some desiccated fossil, the present 200-square-mile salt pan.

Movements of the earth's crust created the valley. In the last five million years—recently, in geologic terms—a series of crustal blocks sank at the same time mountains were lifting around them. The result was a deep, elongated trench. And the warping of the crust persists: Every ten years or so, the valley floor tilts eastward another inch or two.

For almost an hour I walked doggedly across ridges of crusty brown salt and around tough clumps of pickleweed. The sound of fresh water sloshing in bottles inside my pack gave me some sense of security.

Once I had crossed the margin of vegetation, the ground turned

"wonders that represent . . . the great diversity of the continent's geography"

From Greenland, the world's biggest island, to California's giant sequoias, the largest living things, North America's wonders rival all others. The greatest tidal variation anywhere occurs in the Bay of Fundy; the Everglades contains one of the largest mangrove forests on earth; and Superior covers a bigger area—31,700 square miles—than any other freshwater lake. A continent of immense variety, North America holds plains, deserts, mountain ranges, and one of the world's longest river systems—the Mississippi.

*U*behebe—"basket in the earth"—Shoshone Indians called this 500-foot-deep crater in Death Valley National Monument, California. Created by an explosion of hot gases perhaps as recently as a thousand years ago, mineral-streaked Ubehebe carries Little Hebe on its shoulder. Death Valley's deepest point lies 282 feet below sea level—the lowest spot in the Americas.

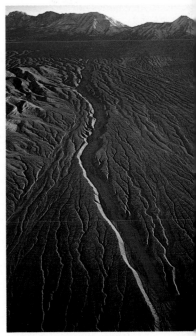

Braided arroyos etch the valley floor (above), which receives a scant 1½ inches of rain annually. In this sun-heated furnace, temperatures sometimes reach 130°F.

143

white—the white of sodium chloride several inches thick. As I moved across this bleached salt flat, my feet often broke through the crust and sank into sucking mud underneath. It was like slogging through wet snow, a fanciful image that melted rapidly in my mind as the sun climbed higher overhead.

About two miles from my starting point, I reached what I figured by the map to be minus 282 feet. I stood there in the middle of a dazzling sea of salt. For some time now I had been talking out loud to myself, like some mad prospector trying to keep himself company.

Then my words suddenly seemed to evaporate. I fell silent. I remembered that scientists refer to the salt pan as a "chemical desert." Nothing but bacteria could live in this salt-saturated environment. It was eerie to stand in such a barren place. Death Valley could have been a crater on the moon. Despite my growing uneasiness, the intensity of the situation held me in fascination. I stood for what seemed a long time until sweat began to blur my sight and the whiteness around me became a threatening form of unconsciousness. Quickly I found my way back to minus 260 feet.

After the harsh aridity of the Southwest, I experienced another extreme—the humid subtropical climate of southwestern Florida, where one of the world's largest mangrove forests grows. Water seems to be everywhere. Tides carry salt water east from the Gulf of Mexico, and a vast sheet of fresh water drains from the 4,000-square-mile saw-grass wetland known as the Everglades. Vegetation chokes the riverbanks, often blocking out the sun. The sudden movement of an animal—a Louisiana

Wings spread out to dry, an anhinga perches on a pond apple tree in Everglades National Park, most extensive subtropical wilderness in the United States. Draining some 4,000 square miles, the vast wetland harbors a profusion of waterfowl and other wildlife. Below, a string of canoes threads a mangrove maze near the park's northwestern boundary.

heron, perhaps, or an alligator—ripples the calm. The atmosphere vibrates with swarming insects and intense heat.

I joined a canoeing party that was heading into the dense mangrove forest. Our route stretched 105 miles down the Gulf coast along the western edge of Everglades National Park. It took us across broad, wind-chopped bays and down narrow, overgrown rivers. Red mangroves

explained, as we talked in Washington, D. C., before my departure for the region. "Sometimes the blizzards are simply windstorms whipping loose snow and ice crystals into blinding horizontal barrages, while a hundred feet above the surface the sun is shining in a pure blue sky.

"But sometimes, when the air is still and the sun is bright, you can look out across the endless shimmering whiteness to the peaks glistening with snow, and the raw beauty and the great silence are overwhelming. It's so quiet you can hear the blood pulsing in your ears."

There is nothing commonplace about earth's coldest, windiest, driest continent. A sense of adventure accompanies any journey there. My trip to a small corner of the Antarctic Peninsula began in South America, where, as a guest of the Chilean Air Force, I boarded a military transport in Punta Arenas, on the Strait of Magellan. My official escort was vivacious Lucía Ramírez Aranda. A four-hour flight took us above the islands of Tierra del Fuego, past Cape Horn, and 500 miles across stormy Drake Passage to the Chilean base in the South Shetland Islands, 70 miles northwest of the peninsula.

As the plane descended, we looked for a break in the thick clouds to give us our first glimpse of the Antarctic. Suddenly we saw a coastal cliff of sheer ice and the blue-white glare of ice floes adrift on the inky blackness of the sea. Fangs of rock rose straight ahead and, with a surge of power, the engines zoomed us back into the clouds. Twice more the pilot tried for a landing, maneuvering through heavy clouds and patches of fog before the plane was finally lined up with the runway.

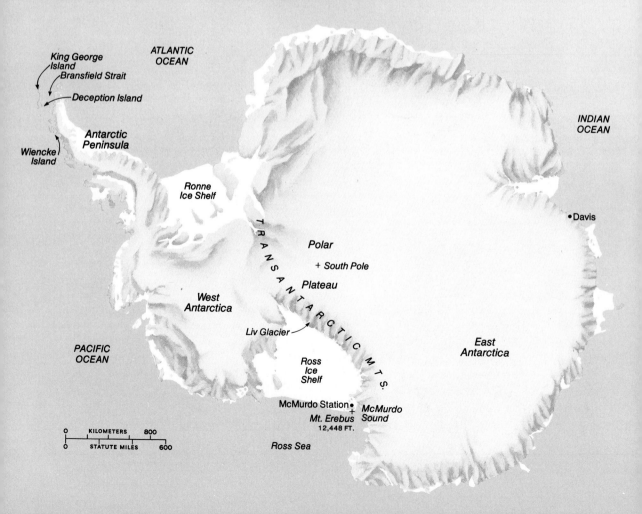

I stepped out on King George Island—and into the incessant wind. Snow patterned the dark slopes on either side of the runway. Pale green lichens and brighter green mosses provided tinges of color in a gray-and-

Luminous curtain across the evening sky, an aurora australis pulsates above Davis, an Australian station on the coast of East Antarctica. Colors in this curled band aurora indicate geomagnetic disturbances 60 to 70 miles up in the earth's atmosphere. Scientists study auroras and other phenomena at some 30 year-round stations. An international treaty, ratified in 1961, sets aside the continent for peaceful purposes such as research in biology, geology, and oceanography.

white world. The island, largest of the South Shetlands, has a relatively moderate climate for the Antarctic, and its ice sheet, hundreds of feet deep in the interior, recedes from the coastal areas in summer.

Along the stony beach stood a dozen penguins. From time to time, one would waddle a little way—with the clumsy, comic gait people find so charming—and hop into the water. Less familiar to me were the speed and grace with which these flightless birds swim, arcing in and out of the water like miniature porpoises, using their wings as powerful flippers.

On my first walk I was startled by attacking brown skuas. The large birds dived repeatedly at me, veering away only inches from my head, and screeching all the while in obvious fury. They were simply being protective parents, for I had inadvertently come too close to their nest.

Skuas, like other antarctic creatures, show little or no fear of people. The Weddell and elephant seals lying on the beaches barely stirred as I came near; they occasionally lifted their heads in indolent curiosity.

Fog, formed when warm, moist air from the north meets the cold Antarctic landmass, blankets coastal areas for long periods in summer, and it had grounded the planes and helicopters at the Chilean base on King George Island. But the cruise ship *World Discoverer*, specially built for antarctic expeditions, was anchored offshore, and Lucía and I were invited aboard for a five-day voyage across the Bransfield Strait and down the icebound coast of the Antarctic Peninsula.

On the way we stopped at Deception Island, an active volcano of black and burnt-red rock capped with ice made gray and gritty by volcanic dust and ash. Thousands, perhaps millions, of years ago, the cone had collapsed, forming a caldera that was invaded by the sea. Today the submerged caldera holds a circular bay several miles across. The ship nosed through Neptune's Bellows, the single narrow channel leading into the bay, and we found ourselves above *(Continued on page 134)*

"earth's coldest, windiest, driest continent"

Remote, icebound, and brutally cold, Antarctica ranks as earth's most alien region, where temperatures sometimes plunge lower than those on Mars. Ice shelves hug the coastline. Formed by snow accumulations over a period of 20 million years, the Antarctic ice sheet covers 98 percent of the continent and reaches a maximum thickness of 16,000 feet. Its weight has depressed the continent by an average of 2,000 feet; most of the landmass lies below sea level.

FRANCISCO ERIZE/BRUCE COLEMAN LTD. (BELOW); RICK RIDGEWAY (ABOVE); CYNTHIA RUSS RAMSAY, N.G.S. STAFF (OPPOSITE); EDMUND STUMP/N.S.F. (FOLLOWING PAGES)

Climbers leave crusty tracks on Wiencke Island in the Palmer Archipelago off the Antarctic Peninsula. At volcanic Deception Island (opposite), a cruise ship anchors in the bay filling a caldera. Steaming water heated by submerged fumaroles entices bathers on the cinder beach.

Overleaf: Sea ice grinding relentlessly against land creates jagged pressure ridges along the Ross Sea coast. Beyond them, steam drifts from 12,448-foot Mount Erebus, the world's southernmost active volcano.

the drowned heart of the still steaming crater. Several eruptions have occurred here within the past 20 years, including one in 1969 that destroyed a British base.

In Zodiacs—rubber boats—we headed for the cinder beach, overwhelmingly bleak beneath the heavy gray sky. Plumes of steam, as if from some immense witch's caldron, curled upward along the shore, where the earth's hidden fires heated the sea and permitted a novel dip in Antarctic waters for an intrepid few.

"It's scalding directly above a fumarole," said one bather, constantly stirring the water to produce a tolerable mix of hot and cold.

D eception Island is not the only volcanic wonder in Antarctica. Some 2,500 miles away, steam wafts from the crater of Mount Erebus, the 12,448-foot volcano that looms over McMurdo Station.

Our other ports of call were an Argentine and a Chilean installation on the Antarctic Peninsula itself. Both are perched on narrow strips of land protruding from the ice.

As we cruised along, I found it hard to believe that Antarctica had not always been frozen. Scientists theorize that this landmass was once part of a warmer supercontinent called Pangaea that broke apart. Fossil remains of a number of extinct reptiles that flourished more than 200 million years ago in South Africa and India were found in the Transantarctic Mountains in 1969. And in 1982 the fossil jawbone of a marsupial that lived 40 million years ago was discovered on an island off the Antarctic Peninsula. Scientists think the discovery provides proof that marsupials originating in South America dispersed across Antarctica to Australia. Both finds support the theory that at one time the southern continents were connected.

Overhead in the pale midnight sky, black-and-white gulls and dainty Antarctic terns soared on the wind. Birdlife abounds in this white world, feeding on the plankton and fishes that teem in the frigid waters.

Icebergs carved by wind and waves provided a gallery of abstract sculptures. But nothing made us scramble to the decks faster than the captain's announcement that whales were off the port bow. At first we saw only a geyser of spray—a whale's spout. Then two massive humpbacks appeared, breaching and slapping their flukes with resounding splashes. Three times the whales vanished, only to reappear on the other side of the ship, awing us with their sleek power.

Until recently, many species of whales in these southern waters were being hunted nearly to extinction. Today, international quota agreements limit the number of kills, and only the Soviet Union, Japan, and Brazil still engage in commercial whaling here.

Now other resources of the Antarctic are attracting attention. Several nations have begun harvesting shrimplike krill, which swarm in the millions, turning the ocean orange-pink. Geologists have located vast amounts of coal, and speculate that the region may also hold deposits of oil, natural gas, and various ores.

The future may bring efforts to exploit this wealth, and advanced technology may yet make further conquests in Antarctica. But many people all over the world want the continent to remain a pristine laboratory for scientific research. The challenge may come as mineral and food shortages grow more compelling. Perhaps, though, the frozen continent is so formidable that it will defy and defeat any assault.

" 'the raw beauty and the great silence are overwhelming' "

Rivulets of meltwater furrow the Ross Ice Shelf near McMurdo Sound. Chunks of ice, coated with salt deposits, bear rocky debris carried by glaciers from the Transantarctic Mountains. At the rate of several inches an hour, the ice shelf moves toward the open sea, where it calves to form icebergs. Largest ice shelf in the world, it covers 200,000 square miles. More than 2,000 feet thick in places, the shelf floats like a raft on the great wedge of sea between East and West Antarctica.

GEORG GERSTER

North America

By Thomas O'Neill

Photographs by
Georg Gerster

P resident Theodore Roosevelt called it "one of the great sights which every American . . . should see." Following the road signs, I drove across sagebrush desert and through forests of ponderosa pine. A marker indicated that I had only a mile to go. I stopped the car and began to walk. The horizon revealed nothing. Suddenly the ground fell away below me, and I found myself looking into the most astounding abyss that nature has to offer. I fumbled for a brochure and read some numbers: The Grand Canyon in northwest Arizona is 277 miles long, from 600 feet to 18 miles wide, and as much as a mile deep.

These figures could not begin to convey the overwhelming spectacle and scale of the canyon, the largest in the world. Below me lay an immense gash in the earth's surface, broad enough to encompass a seemingly endless succession of peaks and buttes. It was as if a mountain range had once been buried within the earth and had slowly reemerged.

Geologist Clarence Dutton, who studied the Grand Canyon from 1875 to 1881 and named many of its features, marveled at the profusion of rock formations, especially the buttes. "There are scores of these structures," he wrote, "any one of which, if it could be placed by itself upon some distant plain, would be regarded as one of the great wonders of the world. Yet here they crowd each other. . . . [and] the power and grandeur is quite beyond description."

The canyon was changing colors in the late afternoon. First the rocks glowed orange and yellow as if a furnace burned inside. Then, as the sun sank lower, the walls turned a fiery red like live embers. Finally the rocks cooled and a deep purple stole over them as night fell.

Far below, a ribbon of green flecked with white appeared here and there in the inner gorge. It was the Colorado River, master builder of the canyon. Water cutting rock. For millions of years the Colorado has been steadily slicing through the Kaibab Plateau, creating this chasm. And the canyon keeps getting deeper—at an imperceptible but relentless rate, averaging a few inches every thousand years.

The Grand Canyon is, of course, only one of many natural marvels in North America. From the long list I chose seven wonders that represent for me the great diversity of the continent's geography. Besides the Grand Canyon, my itinerary included Death Valley in California, the Everglades of Florida, the Bay of Fundy between Nova Scotia and New Brunswick, the Columbia Icefield and the Yellowstone geyser fields in the Rocky Mountains, and Mammoth Cave in Kentucky.

Like the other wonders I would visit, the Grand Canyon offers not only stunning scenery but also startling evidence of the workings of

Carved by wind and water, the Double Arch at Arches National Park in eastern Utah soars above a silhouetted visitor. The park's spectacular array of bizarre sandstone formations includes more than 90 arches and scores of other features—domes, windows, natural bridges, and balancing rocks.

Overleaf: Glowing golden in the sunset, buttes and mesas of the Grand Canyon of the Colorado, the world's largest gorge, march to the horizon.

N.G.S. PHOTOGRAPHER GEORGE F. MOBLEY
(OPPOSITE)

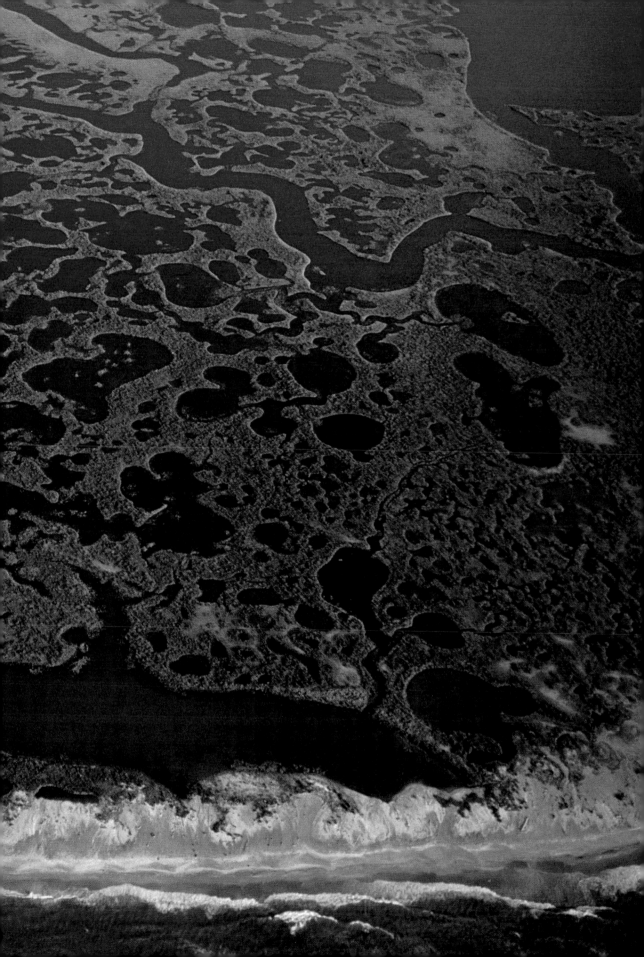

crowded the banks, their large, clawlike prop roots arching down into the muck. We also saw stands of black mangroves, with their short, stalk-like roots that cluster around the trunks and perhaps serve as breathing tubes. Because they can tolerate salt water, mangroves thrive as no other plants do in this brackish estuary.

We were never alone. Ospreys dove into the water from 50 feet up to snatch fish in their talons. Tall, gangling herons stood still as statues along the shadowy banks. Cormorants took off across the water, skimming the surface like skipping rocks. White ibises squawked and thrashed in the treetops. Wood storks made a din in a rookery hidden behind an island. Now and then we sighted sinuous, ancient-looking alligators swimming methodically in open water.

We came to a section known as "Nightmare" on our fifth day out. It was a dank, tortuous tunnel running through the forest. Tangled mangrove roots seemed to clutch at our canoes. Birds peered down from branches like gargoyles, and the sulfurous odor of decomposing vegetation rose from the murky water. We were glad to emerge.

Ever since people began coming in large numbers to southern Florida more than a century ago, land drainage, irrigation, flood control, and the demand for drinking water have combined to reduce drastically the amount of water that once flowed south through the Everglades and maintained its complex ecosystem.

"Ten times as much water probably flowed into the Everglades years ago," Park Superintendent Jack Morehead told me. "The freshwater wading bird population has declined more than 90 percent since the early 1900s. The fishery resources have also declined dramatically, and we're seeing an invasion of nonindigenous plant species."

Faced with these disturbing developments, Morehead and his staff are studying ways to restore a more natural water flow to the park to save its wildlife. The latest recommendations call for at least doubling the amount of water now being released into the park by Florida's Water Management Districts. The additional amount, planners say, could come from water currently being flushed unused into the Atlantic Ocean as part of the flood control program. The park proposal also asks that the water be delivered in a way that would simulate the wet and dry seasons rather than being released erratically, as it is now.

"I don't expect a return to the natural system simply because people are here to stay in south Florida," Superintendent Morehead emphasized. "We have to prevent floods, and we have to provide water for agriculture and urban development. It's obvious: The same amount of water is not available any more."

Our group proceeded gingerly at times through the mangrove forest, anxious to leave no trace of our passage. Once we traveled at night. We had been trying to sleep on a chickee—an open-sided, thatch-roofed platform above the water, modeled after a Seminole Indian camp. A storm of mosquitoes drove us back into our canoes, and we glided out into the darkness. Fog hung like gauze over the water; I could barely see the shadowy outline of the canoe next to mine. As we paddled, our canoes left wakes made silvery by phosphorescent organisms in the water. We called to each other to keep our bearings. We enjoyed traveling that way—ghost-like, with a shimmering trail that disappeared as soon as we had passed.

Overleaf: Fragile Chandeleur Islands in the Mississippi Delta region of Louisiana battle the surging surf of the Gulf of Mexico. Vestiges of a former delta abandoned when the Mississippi changed course 600 years ago, these barrier islands now migrate westward as much as 30 feet a year. Elsewhere, erosion annually claims about 50 square miles of Louisiana's coastal areas, imperiling some of North America's finest wetlands.

148

The movement of water, essential to the existence of the Grand Canyon and the Everglades, also accounts for the uniqueness of Canada's Bay of Fundy, my next stop. The bay has phenomenal tides, the greatest in the world. The difference between high and low water is as much as 53 feet. Every 12 hours and 25 minutes, moon-driven tides from the Atlantic Ocean pile into the Bay of Fundy between Nova Scotia and New Brunswick. Up the inlet's 170-mile length rushes the lifting water, generating waves as high as six feet, carving boulders into fanciful shapes, and reversing the flow of the St. John River.

Fishermen and tourists alike schedule their activities by the tides. Stores sell tide tables alongside food and clothes. No one who uses the water in any way can ignore the lunar day of 24 hours and 50 minutes. As one 20-year inhabitant of the Fundy region told me, "We've all gone aground at one time or another, cutting things too fine."

In the small coastal town of St. Andrews, New Brunswick, I would walk out on the wharf in the evening and watch the tide go out. The water would slowly draw back, revealing yard after yard of glistening mud flats filigreed with purple seaweed and dotted with feeding gulls. For six hours the retreat would go on, until the boats I could have boarded from the dock lay far below me, tilted awkwardly in the mud.

The Mic-Mac Indians, who once lived on the Fundy coast, attributed these tides to the giant Glooscap, who sat down to take a bath in a trench dug for him by a beaver. When the clean Glooscap stood up, the water sloshed back and forth, and the giant tides were born.

"phenomenal tides, the greatest in the world"

Left low and dry by the Bay of Fundy's ebb, a fishing boat sits on the mud at Parrsboro Wharf, Nova Scotia. The bay's funnel shape and the water's swaying motion produce the world's greatest tidal variation, averaging more than 40 feet between high and low water. Once, in 1869, it reached a record 103 feet at Burntcoat Head, Nova Scotia.

Modern-day inhabitants prefer to attribute the tides to the bay's funnel-like shape. The bay begins to narrow past its mouth, compressing the incoming tide to greater and greater heights until the water squeezes into two small basins at the head of the bay. It is here that the record 53-foot tides have been measured. The length and contour of the bay are such that the falling tide sweeps out into the ocean just as the rising tide begins to push back in. This creates "resonance," a pulse that gives the bay the perpetually swaying rhythm necessary for enormous tides.

People have constantly sought to put these tides to use. Fishermen have had the greatest success. Adopting an efficient Indian method, they construct large fish traps called weirs out of brush, net, and stakes. The traps catch fish that are returning from coastal feeding areas to deep water at high tide. Most weir fishing is done at the mouth of the bay, where tides average about 20 feet. At the time of my visit, 270 weirs

*M*ud flats glisten as the
sun sets at low tide on
Chignecto Bay, an arm
of the Bay of Fundy. Rootlike patterns
mark the course of streams draining
into the bay. The fast-flowing water
gnaws at the base of rocks, leaving
tree-capped "flowerpots" (top),
arches (above), and caves.
The powerful tides have inspired
hydroelectric schemes in which
dams generate electricity as falling
tidewater sluices through turbines.

were being fished, mostly for juvenile herring, sold as sardines. Fishing was poor at the mouth in early summer, however, and I moved up to the head of the bay on the Nova Scotia side, where I found Gerald Lewis.

I hopped aboard his horse-drawn cart as it left a stony beach near the small town of Five Islands. With the tide out, we crossed a soggy mud flat, tinted red by clay eroded from the cliffs along the shore. In the distance, pairs of people hunched in the mud and dug for clams.

Gerald is a friendly, weathered man who has lived all his life near the Fundy shore. Since boyhood, Gerald has fished a weir for large, silvery shad. "When I took over the weir a while back, it had been used in this same spot for 113 years," he told me as we rolled along.

After a time, we reached the weir, which stretched out to a length of 2,500 feet. Noisy gulls and cormorants perched on the 12-foot-high stakes—a sign that there were fish in the trap at the foot of the weir. Gerald unwound a small seining net, dragged it through the shallow pool, and came up with a dozen shad.

"I was hoping for more, but I guess the water is too cold. A good run is seven hundred, eight hundred, even a thousand fish. You'd get dizzy watching," Gerald said wistfully. He'd be back in 12 hours and 25 minutes to try again.

Fundy's tides have tempted people to harness them for energy. Since the early years of this century, plans have been proposed for building tidal dams that would generate great amounts of power simply by sluicing water through turbines as the tide dropped. I visited a small tidal power demonstration plant under construction in the bay, at the mouth of Nova Scotia's Annapolis River, the first project of its kind in North America. A monolithic concrete powerhouse stood in place with two 50-foot-square openings ready to receive the surging tides. The project

"O hushed October morning mild, Thy leaves have ripened to the fall," wrote poet Robert Frost of autumn in his beloved New England. Early reds and golds appear on Vermont's forested hills (far right), soon to ignite into a blazing mass of color. Brilliantly hued maple leaves (right) help make fall in the northeastern United States one of nature's most resplendent spectacles.

Following pages: A collapsed volcano that erupted some 6,800 years ago cups Crater Lake in Oregon's Cascade Range. Over the millennia rain and snowmelt filled the 20-square-mile basin to its present level of 1,932 feet, making this the second deepest lake in North America; Canada's Great Slave Lake surpasses it by 83 feet.

engineer told me that the turbine would arrive soon on a barge from Montreal, and the plant would be in operation within a year.

The plant will contain just the one turbine and produce 20,000 kilowatts of electricity. It's a mere toy compared with other plants being envisioned. Designs exist for an immense one with 128 turbines and a dam five miles long that would generate almost five million kilowatts, more than double the energy produced by all of Nova Scotia's oil- and coal-fired plants. The dam would be in the Minas Basin, where the tides reach 50 feet, a few miles above Gerald Lewis's weir.

I headed west again, back across the continent to the Rocky Mountains, where by early July most of the snow had melted from the high valleys and slopes. Mountains dominate the western third of North America, and the Rockies make up its largest chain, extending 1,900 miles from New Mexico to British Columbia. I stopped in the rugged northwest corner of Wyoming, where someone told me a story about a volcanic eruption:

"In the more than four billion years of the earth's history, the eruption was one of the biggest geologic catastrophes we know of. The explosion was a thousand times greater than Mount St. Helens. In just a few hours, hundreds of thousands of cubic feet of hot ash were ejected. Deposits have been found in Canada, Mexico, and northern Mississippi. When the volcanic dome collapsed, it left a caldera 28 miles across. There were lava flows and searing clouds of gas. Remember, all of this was happening when large glaciers may have been coming out of the mountains. Imagine the meeting of fire and ice. Wow!"

Geologist John Good fell silent. Perhaps he was visualizing the enormous, blinding cloud of steam created when the heat of the volcano

met the cold of the glaciers. "Wow!" he repeated softly. We were sitting in his office, only a few miles from the rim of that gigantic caldera in Yellowstone National Park. The eruption had occurred here almost 600,000 years before. The caldera is mostly disguised now, mantled with forests and meadows, filled in by lava that has seeped up through fissures in the ground.

Clouds of steam still roll over Yellowstone. They come from geysers, hot springs, mud volcanoes, and fumaroles, evidence of the tremendous heat flow that still exists beneath this part of the continent.

I walked in the park, and underneath me, less than four miles down, lay molten rock. Rocks in the earth's upper mantle and lower crust have partially melted and flowed upward, forming a spacious magma chamber in the crust. In many areas of North America, molten material lies as far as 20 miles beneath the surface. But here in Yellowstone, the magma is close enough to the surface to boil groundwater circulating through the rocks. Steam pressure propels the scalding water up through cracks and along fault lines, creating spectacular thermal activity. Scientists theorize that the magma chamber is a hot spot in the earth's mantle that the continental plate is passing over, or else that the hot rocks exist at the leading edge of a fault line that is opening like a zipper.

"It helps if you think of Yellowstone as a condition, not as an area,"

Old Faithful explodes in a tower of superheated steam at Upper Geyser Basin, in Yellowstone National Park, Wyoming. More than 140 geysers vent the earth's inner heat in an area of less than one square mile, the greatest concentration of geysers in the world. The Gumper (below), a steaming mud pot nearly 70 feet across, boils and bubbles in another section of the park.

John Good advised me. "And that condition is moving slowly to the northeast. Fifteen million years ago, the hot spot existed beneath the place where Boise, Idaho, is today. In another five million years, you may find it where Billings, Montana, is now."

Yellowstone contains the world's largest geyser field—some 300 geysers in all, with spouts 3 to 380 feet high. The most celebrated one, of course, is Old Faithful. Others shoot higher, but none is so regular and so dramatic at the same time. It has been blowing, on an average, every 65 minutes for more than 100 years. Before one eruption, I saw hundreds

*A*lgae tint the muddy banks of Yellowstone's Grand Prismatic Spring, whose waters steam at 150°F. An aerial view (opposite) reveals the extraordinary coloration of the heart-shaped spring. A boardwalk, at lower right, takes visitors close to the edge of the 370-foot-wide pool. After leaving the Lewis and Clark Expedition in 1806, fur trapper John Colter may have become the first white American to explore the Yellowstone region; his descriptions of its "gloomy terrors, its hidden fires, smoking pits, noxious streams" earned it the nickname "Colter's Hell." Later expeditions reported "scenery surpassing in grandeur anything . . . before seen." In 1872 Congress established Yellowstone as the United States' first national park, now visited by more than two and a half million people every year.

of summer tourists pack the benches in front of the crater and sit there politely, as if waiting for a concert to begin. Suddenly steam came pumping furiously out of Old Faithful, as superheated water underground began to release pressure. With a locomotive's roar, the earth hurled up a white tower of water, fountaining higher and higher until it reached 130 feet. The performance lasted about a minute; the audience applauded.

Two glaciers inch past Mount Shackleton (above), high on the roof of the Canadian Rockies, part of the continent's mightiest mountain chain. On the slope of Snow Dome (opposite), crevasses riddle the Athabasca Glacier as it creeps down from the Columbia Icefield over buried bedrock cliffs. Meltwater from the many glaciers on the 110-square-mile icefield discharges into three oceans—Atlantic, Pacific, and Arctic.

In the northern section of the park, hot springs have deposited mounds of travertine that resemble terraced temples. At another spot, mud craters—"no deeper than a hog wallow," according to a park interpreter—bubble like caldrons. One mud pot, fondly known as the Gumper, appeared almost overnight in 1974, possibly as a result of one of the 200 tremors that strike Yellowstone each year. Now the Gumper is almost 70 feet across and splatters trees 30 feet away.

At the Norris Geyser Basin, I saw geysers spout from land where nothing can grow because the water is so acidic. Visitors were keeping a vigil at nearby Steamboat, the largest geyser in the world. Its gushes reach 380 feet—higher than the Statue of Liberty. But it is unpredictable. When I was there, it was erupting every 11 to 14 days. I talked with people who had been waiting eight hours, hoping for The Moment.

From the fires of Yellowstone, I journeyed north to a realm of ice— the Columbia Icefield in the Canadian Rockies, astride the British Columbia-Alberta border. From a snowy plateau 10,000 feet high, a dozen glaciers spill down into deep mountain valleys. One of them, the Athabasca, comes down almost to the highway at the southern end of Jasper National Park, where I was staying.

On a July morning, I set out with Dan Young, a geologist from Edmonton, to hike up Saskatchewan Glacier. Almost six miles long, it is the largest glacier in the icefield. As we headed toward the enormous tongue of ice, a chalk-colored stream rushed furiously past us in its gravel bed. The glacier was melting on this warm day, releasing a heavy flow of water from tunnels at its snout. The tiny stream marked the beginning

of the North Saskatchewan River, which runs through three provinces and into Hudson Bay, 1,600 miles away.

We approached the glacier from its side, scrambling over a 19th-century moraine of inactive ice covered with rocks that had fallen from the valley walls and had been deposited in a huge pile as the glacier slid past. A century ago the glacier had reached the top of the moraine, but now the ice lay 400 feet below us. Since 1870 the Saskatchewan Glacier, like all but one on the icefield, has been shrinking.

From the moraine we descended to the edge of the glacier, where a wild meltwater stream was tossing boulders along as if they were cobbles. After vaulting the water, we cut steps in the ice with our axes and climbed the slope to the top of the glacier. The surface was alive with water. Every 15 feet or so, torrents of icewater rushed down the glacier. Where the channels reached a fracture in the ice, they poured into the interior of the glacier, the swirling motion of the falling water cutting deep cylindrical wells called moulins.

"Welcome to the time warp," Dan had remarked when we first looked at the icefield. Now, as we neared the head of the glacier in a stark landscape of ice and rock, I understood what he meant. This river of ice belonged in my mind to a time thousands of years ago when massive ice sheets scraped down the continent, radically reshaping the land. Up here on the roof of the Rockies, we had crossed into the Ice Age.

It's strange to think of a massive wedge of ice moving beneath you, but move it does, at an average rate of 85 feet a year. Snow piles up on the plateau above, crystallizing into ice under the weight of accumulated falls. The force of gravity begins to drag the ice down into the valleys. Ice-watching is not for the impatient, I learned. It takes about 500 years from the time a snowflake falls on the icefield to the time it appears as an ice crystal on the snout of the Saskatchewan Glacier.

After walking about four hours, we reached the top of the glacier. The sky had clouded over, and we shivered in the wind as we gazed upon

a primitive scene in black and white. That night, after we had hiked off, I stared a long while out my hotel window at the Athabasca Glacier across the road. It gleamed dully in the late evening light, like a fish pulled out of water. With all the jagged fractures on its surface, the glacier seemed to be straining to escape from the prison of its valley.

I ended my North American journey in west-central Kentucky, at a place about halfway between Louisville and Nashville, Tennessee. The woods here are thick, towns are small, with names like Pig and Uno, and cattle graze in sinkholes. It seems an unlikely area in which to conclude a tour of the continent's natural wonders. But the attraction here does not lie on the surface. It lies underground, in at least 235 miles of subterranean passages.

Mammoth Cave is the longest known cave system in the world. It is nearly three times longer than the runner-up, a 90-mile system called Optimistitscheskaja, in the Soviet Union. To descend into the dark, cool depths of Mammoth is to discover an extraordinary wilderness of stalactites and stalagmites, corridors up to 100 feet high, miles-long tubular passages, narrow canyons, water-drenched shafts and crawlways.

Mammoth Cave owes its existence to the plateau of pure, thick limestone that extends across the Kentucky countryside. For at least a million years, large amounts of rainwater and meltwater have seeped through openings in the rock, mostly through sinkholes. The water gathers into underground rivers and streams that flow along fractures in the limestone beds, hollowing out a honeycomb of passages as they go. The water eventually discharges into the Green River, a tributary of the Ohio. As the Green River has eroded downward, the underground flows have kept pace, continually dropping and leaving behind a labyrinth of varying levels. And Mammoth Cave keeps growing. Below the ancient upper passages, water, that most proficient of engineers, continues to dissolve tunnels through solid rock.

"an extraordinary wilderness of stalactites and stalagmites"

Deep within Kentucky's ancient limestones, a spelunker twists past water-sculptured formations in Mammoth Cave (above and opposite), the world's longest known cave system—extending at least 235 miles.

Overleaf: In a midnight time exposure, Mount McKinley, or Denali—at 20,320 feet North America's highest peak—looms above Alaskan wilderness.

Like other wonders I had seen, Mammoth Cave offers the chance for adventure. But what makes Mammoth especially exciting is that parts of it now being explored probably have never been seen before.

Prehistoric Indians were the first people to poke into Mammoth Cave, more than 3,000 years ago. Cane torches, slippers made of vegetable fiber, and two mummified bodies have been found far from the entrances where the Indians camped. White men discovered the cave system in the late 1700s, and by the mid-19th century it had become one of the most ballyhooed tourist attractions in the United States. Period illustrations show men in frock coats and women in bonnets and long skirts hiking sturdily through the dark underworld.

Exploration became systematic only in the late 1950s, with the formation of the Cave Research Foundation. Composed of volunteer cavers and scientists and headquartered in Washington, D. C., the CRF supports research in caves throughout the world. The largest of its four field operations is in Mammoth Cave National Park. In 1972, a CRF survey team captured international attention when it discovered a connection between the 86-mile Flint Ridge cave system and the 58-mile Mammoth system, thereby establishing Mammoth as earth's longest cave complex. More than 90 miles have since been added to the total.

One summer weekend, 25 CRF cavers converged on Mammoth Cave National Park to continue the foundation's ambitious project of mapping the entire network. The outing attracted a typically diverse group of people, but all alike in their almost childlike enthusiasm for scrambling around in caves.

I joined Tom Alfred, John Branstetter, and Terry Leitheuser on a mission to redo an old survey line and see what we could find. To reach the survey area we walked through the main section of Mammoth Cave, with its cavernous rooms and its nine miles of electrically lighted trails. We soon plunged into a deep darkness broken only by the cones of light from the carbide lamps on our helmets. Two of us stretched the metal measuring tape, while another read the compass, and another took down numbers and sketched the passageways.

When we reached the last of the survey points, we understood why a previous party had turned back. Facing us was an opening about three feet high and two feet wide with water glistening beyond it. We never considered stopping. The four of us squirmed through the opening and sloshed through cold, shallow water on our hands and knees. The water fell to another level after a while, and we could stand hunchbacked on the rim of a small, zigzagging canyon.

"Feel that air," said John, referring to the constant breeze. "This has to lead to a real cave." We moved on, and the tighter and wetter the passageway became, the more our excitement grew. We had been underground more than six hours and hadn't stood up straight nearly all that time. We came to another tight canyon with hardly enough room in which to turn our heads. Then we stopped. A boulder blocked our way.

"Where we've been today has to be virgin cave," Tom Alfred finally whispered. "No one's been here before."

So there we half-stood, 300 feet underground, cold, mud-coated, bone-sore, hungry. And we grinned. It was a strangely wonderful place—as dramatic and rewarding in its way as the floor of the Grand Canyon, the peaks of the Rockies, the rivers of the Everglades.

"Stunning scenery... startling evidence of the workings of nature"

At the feet of forest titans, two visitors to Sequoia National Park play in the shadow of earth's largest living things. The giant sequoias, some of them more than 250 feet tall and 100 feet around, grow only on the western slopes of California's Sierra Nevada. They can attain ages of 3,000 years and more, owing their longevity in part to their fire-resistant bark.

South America

By Loren McIntyre
Photographs by the Author

"**P**ink flashes of gunfire blossomed along the green wall of trees that crowded the banks of the Amazon." So began my first attempt at writing an adventure story when I was a schoolboy in Seattle long ago. Somewhat later I urged an early love to run away with me to Lake Titicaca, where we would sail romantically into the sunset.

In those days I knew little about South America and the wonders I was daydreaming about. Now the most remote source lake of the Amazon bears my name, and I have sailed into scores of Titicaca sunsets. And yet I keep seeking magical places on the continent that captured my boyhood fancy. I journey there again and again to rediscover its natural marvels—the Amazon and the Rio Negro, Angel Falls and Iguazú Falls, the Atacama Desert, Lake Titicaca, peaks in the Andes—all of them magical to me.

I first sailed the Amazon as a teenager on a cargo ship in 1935. From the Brazilian city of Belém at the river's mouth I wrote home about a pet monkey named Jocko and a boa constrictor I bought in the waterfront market. I found the letter in my attic the other day, yellowed and worn from my father's showing it to friends in those years of the Great Depression, when few could travel abroad and fellows my age were vagabonding around the United States in railroad boxcars. Reading it 48 years later, I realized how much that Amazon experience has shaped my life.

Over the years I have traveled all of the dozen or so major tributaries of the Amazon, as well as some of the thousand lesser streams that join to make the Amazon the world's mightiest river, its volume exceeding the combined flow of the next eight largest rivers. But not until June and July 1982 did I make the ultimate trip—into one of the few regions of the Amazon basin that are still virtually untouched by humankind.

In a 30-foot aluminum cabin cruiser, I ascended 650 miles of the Rio Negro from Manaus, in Brazil, to a point near the Brazil-Colombia-Venezuela intersect. The craft was skippered by inventor Jim Helbig and his wife, Liz; they had built it themselves in Denver, Colorado, and shipped it to South America. A fourth member of our crew was Karen Dreste, a geology student from New York City.

An enormous stygian stream laced with heavily forested islands, the Rio Negro has a volume of flow greater than that of any other river on earth except the Amazon, into which it pours just below Manaus. And to that confluence the Rio Negro at high water sometimes brings a greater volume than the Amazon itself. This giant tributary is 10 or more miles wide in some places and 300 feet deep in others.

It was the rainy season, and the Rio Negro was so deep in parts that

Ghostly arms of a lifeless tree spread above the lush vegetation of the Amazon basin in Brazil. Most extensive rain forest in the world, the huge region encompasses more than two million square miles of wilderness drained by the Amazon River and its many tributaries.

Overleaf: Flooding forested islands to the treetops, the Rio Negro—largest tributary of the Amazon—flows through northern Brazil.

sometimes our electronic depth finder registered scattered signals that we thought indicated schools of fish, until we realized they were being reflected by the leafy crown of a drowned jungle. We joked about piranhas attacking birds' nests in the treetops. Immaculate white sand beaches, where years ago I had moored a floatplane during an exploratory flight, now lay 20 to 30 feet beneath the broad, moving surface.

By day we voyaged so close to the shores of nameless islands that overhanging branches shaded us from the sun. Our prow parted curtains of lianas that trailed like ropes in the black-water current. We never tired of peering into half-submerged forests to see what surprises might lurk behind the tangled vegetation. Orchids and rarer blossoms—and even bats—clung to tree trunks almost within reach.

Of human life we saw but little: some days only a dugout or two and perhaps a one-family house perched on stilts at the tip of an island. Home-seeking colonists from densely populated eastern Brazil have not yet penetrated this watery world. The rapacious hand of man, so widely reported to be cutting down tropical forests, seldom lifts an ax along the Rio Negro and its broad tributaries. According to one settler from whom we bought a loin of wild boar, no tourists had come this way in years except for a Canadian father and son who had canoed down the river.

The most delightful aspect of my Rio Negro trip was the absence of mosquitoes, due, perhaps, to the slight acidity of the water. Not once were we tormented by the notorious swarms of stinging, disease-carrying insects that bring misery to outlanders and aborigines alike in most of the Amazon basin. We could sleep under the stars without netting.

At nightfall we sometimes tied our boat to the top of a sunken tree out in the stream. We risked being torn away by a sudden squall, but thunder always awakened us with a warning to double up our lines and batten down our hatches. And then we would hear the roar of rain approaching through the trees and across the water.

Usually we preferred to moor within one of the thousands of secret inlets—*igarapés* in the Portuguese of Brazil, *caños* in Spanish—that thread aimlessly into the flooded forests. Once among the trees, we had to avoid knocking our heads against wasps' nests, and we sprayed our mooring lines with pesticide to ward off columns of ants that tried to march on board during the night. The inlets lead eventually to stagnant lakes where submerged vegetation steeps in warm, slack water the color of tea. The brew oozes out of the swamps and stains the main stream almost black, giving the Rio Negro its name.

Each day we awakened to the treble melodies of birds and the basso profundo dissonance of howler monkeys. Loudest animal noise in the jungle, the howlers' chorus of roars, heard from two or three miles away, sounds rather like torrential rains approaching.

Halfway up the Rio Negro we sighted outcroppings of rock, rounded masses of granite blackened by weathering. Chipping with her geologist's hammer, Karen collected fragments, black outside, white inside. Currents swirled around the smooth swellings of stone, a preview of cataracts to come. Soon we had to hire Indian rivermen to pilot us through safe passages. Our three-ton aluminum boat had to be revved up to ten knots to get through the worst rapids at São Gabriel da Cachoeira, the only large town on the upper river—where we paid $2,000 for 500 gallons of gasoline.

From jungle flatlands upstream rose isolated granite domes spaced miles apart, monuments to eons of weathering. One such monolith, about 1,200 feet high, marks the Brazilian frontier at the town of Cucuí. A few miles farther north, in San Carlos, in Venezuela, we were joined by Jim's partner, Bob Williams, and Bob's son Hunt. We left the Rio Negro just above San Carlos and turned into the Casiquiare, a unique offshoot of the Orinoco; it links that broad river to the Amazon, making this the only place on earth where two major river systems are connected near their sources by a natural navigable waterway.

Most European mapmakers refused to believe that the Casiquiare linked the two rivers until explorer-naturalist Alexander von Humboldt

Blanketing a third of the continent, the tropical forests of the Amazon basin dominate South America's northern interior. Lacing this immense rain-soaked landscape, the mighty Amazon—by volume the largest river in the world—gains strength from more than 1,000 tributaries on a 4,000-mile journey from the Peruvian Andes to the Atlantic Ocean. The Andes, longest and second highest mountain chain on earth, extend more than 4,000 miles along the western coast. South America also holds spectacular waterfalls, barren deserts, miles-high lakes, and snowcapped volcanoes.

navigated it from one end to the other in 1800. But many Europeans did believe the legend that hidden among vast ranges lay fabulous Lake Parima, on whose silvery shores rose the golden towers of Manoa, a lost city ruled by El Dorado, the Gilded Man. Sir Walter Raleigh searched unsuccessfully for the city in the lower Orinoco region.

Like Raleigh, we found no golden city. But as soon as we left the black-water Rio Negro and entered the brownish Casiquiare, we were

attacked by hordes of gnats and mosquitoes, descendants of the pests that Humboldt complained about in page after page of his journal. Within minutes, Karen counted 167 bites on her arms and hands and then gave up. She quickly followed my example of spraying frequently with insect repellent and taking 500 milligrams of vitamin B_1 a day, which also seems to discourage mosquitoes. The pests perhaps explain why even fewer people live along the Casiquiare now than in Humboldt's day; in nearly 200 miles we saw no more than a score of settlers.

We came out of the Casiquiare and into the Orinoco headwaters near the foot of Mount Duida, at 7,861 feet the highest granite dome of all we saw. Farther downstream we reached the great cataracts of the Orinoco, where the boat had to be portaged 40 miles by trailer. There I left it, while the others voyaged on down the Orinoco and out one of its 50-odd mouths into the Atlantic Ocean. Having begun their odyssey on the Amazon, the Helbigs thus completed a partial circumnavigation of the Guiana Highlands, the northeastern corner of South America that includes northernmost Brazil, Venezuela south of the Orinoco, and all of Guyana, Surinam, and French Guiana.

In the middle of the Guiana Highlands loom many flat-topped mountains, plateaus with near-vertical sides, some more than 9,000 feet high and many miles across. When torrential rains pummel these plateaus, rivulets pour over their edges and drop hundreds, even thousands of feet until they feather into fine spray in the warmer air below.

In 1935 an American soldier of fortune, Jimmy Angel, flew into the canyon of the remote Río Churún, which drains Auyán Tepuí—Devil Mountain—a 12-by-20-mile plateau. He sighted a waterfall that he thought must be the highest in the world and named it after himself. Not until 14 years later did scientists reach the foot of the falls. During a grueling expedition of many weeks—reported in the November 1949 NATIONAL GEOGRAPHIC—surveyors measured the total drop of Angel

Leaving the black water of the Rio Negro, a riverboat heads upstream on the Amazon. Decaying vegetation stains the Rio Negro the color of strong tea (above); silt washed down from the distant Andes turns the Amazon a mocha brown. Downstream, the brown water dominates the black.

Overleaf: Sunlight glances off a partially submerged sandbar in the Rio Negro. Dense rain forest, largely uninhabited, stretches endlessly into the distance.

Falls at 3,212 feet, 20 times higher than Niagara and indeed higher than any other waterfall.

Since Angel Falls is more accessible and more impressive in the second half of the year, at high water, I journeyed there in August, right after my Rio Negro-Orinoco voyage. My guide was "Jungle Rudy" Truffino, a tough, lean Dutchman who runs a comfortable camp at Ucaima, not far from the Canaima airport, and who has been leading explorers to Angel Falls for nearly 30 years. We went by canoe up the Río Carrao and then into the canyon of the Río Churún, which leads to the falls.

Some rapids were so steep and swift that Rudy's Indian crew had to give full throttle to the 40-horsepower outboard motor that propelled our dugout up big waves curling over unseen rocks. At such turbulent times, Rudy and I got out and walked. A nonstop storyteller, he would point out places where this or that riverman had been dashed to death or drowned. All around us towered stone escarpments, their crenellated crests festooned with wisps of waterfalls.

On the third day we reached Rudy's uppermost camp beside the Río Churún. We bathed in cool, amber-colored water and built a crackling fire that night. Next morning we watched for our first sight of Angel Falls. Clouds slowly dissolved under the rising sun, half unveiling the top of the waterfall. From that angle it appeared to pour from the very peak of a mountain in the sky, then vaporize into mist that filled the canyon below.

That night a wished-for rain pounded the roof of our hut. Rudy gleefully shouted above the din that the downpour would fill the fissured plateau of Auyán Tepuí with water that would quickly run off into Angel and lesser falls and put on a fine show. At daybreak we made a splendid climb up a trail of slippery rocks locked in tangles of tree roots and reached a lookout boulder perfect for viewing Jimmy Angel's discovery.

Now we could see that Angel Falls shoots out of channels about 100 feet below the summit. A few hundred feet farther down, the waters disintegrate into spray, yet the power of tons of falling droplets generates a wind that dashed mist into my lens the moment I tried to take a picture. After a 2,648-foot initial vertical drop, the spray gathers in a rockfall at the bottom to form a massive lower waterfall that spills into the Río Churún. This second cataract is included in the 3,212-foot record height of Angel Falls.

While Angel is the highest waterfall in the world, Iguazú, 2,200

Young fisherman maneuvers his dugout among giant Victoria regia lily pads. Plant life flourishes in the warm, humid climate of the Amazon basin. As many as 50 kinds of orchids, such as the fragrant Laelia (above, left), may cling to a single tree. The long, broad leaves of an anthurium (above, right) soak up sunlight that filters through the forest canopy.

BRUNO BARBEY/MAGNUM (OPPOSITE)

179

miles to the south, is the widest—more than two miles from edge to edge. Iguazú is really a many-splendored panoply of waterfalls: Hundreds of cascades leap from openings in the jungle and plunge as much as 265 feet down black cliffs into the gorge of the Río Iguazú, which soon joins the Río Paraná near the Brazil-Argentina-Paraguay intersect.

T he spectacle did not much amaze the Spaniard who discovered Iguazú. Perhaps he was already sated with the wonders of the New World, for he was Álvar Núñez Cabeza de Vaca, one of four survivors of a 300-man expedition into Florida in 1528. He and his companions endured enslavement by Indians and explored northern Mexico and part of what is now Texas. Later named governor of Spanish territories in southern South America, he landed on the Brazilian coast and set out cross-country for Asunción, in Paraguay, in 1541. He reached the Río Iguazú after so many adventures that this is all he had to report about the falls:

"The current of the Yguazú was so strong that the canoes were carried furiously down the river, for near this spot there is a considerable fall, and the noise made by the water leaping down some high rocks into a chasm may be heard a great distance off, and the spray rises two spear throws and more above the fall."

But for me, Iguazú—seen from the Brazilian brink of the gorge or from a helicopter—is the greatest natural audiovisual happening that South America can offer: virgin forests, churning masses of water, and the stupendous roar of the falls. The Río Iguazú makes a sweeping U-turn and fans out among many wooded islands before it takes its awesome plunge. Side channels splinter into hundreds of cascades great and small, while the main channel pours into the head of the gorge called Devil's Throat, similar to the Horseshoe Falls of the Niagara River.

With heavy rains the volume of Iguazú may swell to twice that of Niagara's maximum, yet at times the thunderous cascades may fade to a whisper of mist or even dry up altogether for several days. A freeze in 1975 that destroyed much of Brazil's coffee crop caused thin ice to form on the water beside the jungly banks of the Río Iguazú.

The raw power of the falls at Devil's Throat is accentuated by the delicate flight of thousands of daredevil swifts that flit through rainbows and spray and nest in rocky crevices behind the deluge. The birds arrive at dusk, enter a holding pattern above Devil's Throat, and then dive into the spray singly or in groups. Some circle, and others—when their diving speed matches the velocity of the falling water—zip through momentary breaks in the falls and land on ledges behind the constant thunder. Others alight on the exposed amphitheater of vertical rock and cling there all night long, body to body, forming wet blankets of feathers as much as 50 feet wide. As soon as the morning sunlight touches them, the swifts let go and fly away to catch insects in midair.

Today the falls are protected by national parks on both sides of the Iguazú. Along access roads, Brazilians have put up small green signs characteristic of their conservation efforts: FLORESTA E A CIDADE DOS BICHOS—NAO A DESTRUA (The forest is the city of the wild creatures—Don't destroy it) and ARVORE E IGUAL A GENTE—PRECISA DE CARINHO (Trees are like people—They need love).

While much of the continent is rain-drenched, nearly half the western edge is an absolute desert. Arid sands and cliffs lie hard by the Pacific shore of Peru and northern Chile, a coastal strip so dry that some

"it appeared to pour from the very peak of a mountain in the sky"

Cascading through clouds, Angel Falls plunges 3,212 feet into a remote canyon in the Venezuelan jungle. Earth's highest waterfall, it remained unknown to the outside world until 1935.

Following pages: Cataracts of the Iguazú, the world's widest waterfall, thunder over cliffs stretching more than two miles on the Brazil-Argentina border.

Crest of a sand dune snakes near the coast of Chile in the Atacama Desert—driest in the world. Some parts of the Atacama have had no rainfall in decades. Misshapen rocks cast ragged shadows in the area called the "Valley of the Moon" (above, right). Flash floods caused by infrequent but violent rainstorms have fashioned this desolate landscape.

towns go for years without the minimum precipitation readable on a rain gauge: one tenth of a millimeter, less than the thickness of this page.

Since 1947, when I first went to live in Peru, I had worked and traveled on that desert for a total of more than 5,000 days and nights without ever seeing lightning or hearing thunder. Then in February 1981 a sudden thunderstorm in Chile's Atacama Desert spawned a flash flood that washed out a highway moments after I sped by.

A motorist can easily drive the entire length of the west coast desert along the Pan American Highway. Southbound from the humid forest of Ecuador, you encounter a landscape of sand shortly after entering Peru, and you drive 2,600 dry miles before once again reaching a natural forest, beyond La Serena, in Chile. Along its route, the highway crosses many green oases, 8 to 80 miles apart, each watered by a short river that cascades down from the Andes. Towns and plantations use up most of the water before it can reach the sea.

I once lived in Lima, the capital of Peru and the largest city in this arid region. The five million inhabitants of metropolitan Lima make up half the desert population. In 1535 Francisco Pizarro, the conqueror of the Incas, founded the settlement that became Lima in one of the riverine oases peopled by thousands of Indians. Those first Americans were as advanced as the Spaniards in many ways, but they could not match the military might of the invading Europeans. Today, remains of doomed cultures are scattered over and under the sands in thousands of archaeological sites preserved by the extreme aridity.

The combination of a cold offshore current and a high inland mountain range prevents precipitation on this strip of seaside sands. A

rain-inhibiting temperature inversion—cold, dense air underlying warm air—is caused by the chill, north-flowing Peru, or Humboldt, Current. In addition, the Andean barrier of peaks, four miles high, forces clouds rising from the Amazon basin to drop their moisture on the eastern slopes, thus leaving the western side in a rain shadow.

Longest and second highest mountain range on earth, the Andes hold a rich collection of natural wonders that I have enjoyed exploring despite the cold and the discomfort of breathing rarefied air. Aconcagua, at 22,834 feet the highest mountain in the Western Hemisphere, rises west of Mendoza, in Argentina, near the Chilean border. Towering in solitary splendor, it creates its own formidable microclimate. Although its northwestern approach is not difficult to scale, winds from that side often exceed 100 miles an hour, and the mountain has claimed dozens of victims—not of falls or avalanches, but of cold.

Aconcagua's west and south walls are nearly vertical and very hazardous. To the eastern face clings a steep glacier that creeps from the summit down to 20,000 feet, where the ice breaks off in chunks that hurtle into a deep ravine. In November 1973 I scaled that eastern slope to help bring down the body of an American who had frozen to death there nine months earlier. We found his perfectly preserved, parka-clad body lying exposed to the sun at the foot of the glacier, where gales had blown away the powdery snow that may have blanketed him from time to time during the winter.

Sledding the body down ice and snow (Continued on page 190)   185

*G*usting more than 130
miles an hour, fierce
winds sweep plumes of
snow from the summit
of Aconcagua. Soaring above
surrounding peaks in the Andes
of Argentina, Aconcagua—at
an elevation of 22,834 feet—rules
as the loftiest mountain in the
Western Hemisphere. Eleven
thousand feet below the summit,
a member of author McIntyre's
climbing party approaches

a jagged expanse of melting snow
(above). When storms and sub-
zero temperatures prevail, an
ascent of Aconcagua becomes
a grueling ordeal.

*P*addling a reed boat beneath a brooding sky, an Aymara Indian transports a white llama to the Island of the Sun, where the animal will die in a ritual sacrifice to ensure a good harvest. Legendary birthplace of the Incas, the sacred island (right) rises from Lake Titicaca, which straddles the Peru-Bolivia border nearly 2½ miles above sea level. Runoff from the snow-covered Cordillera Real (opposite) feeds the 3,200-square-mile lake, the world's highest body of water navigable by large ships.

was easy, compared with the agony of carrying it over the shifting ash on the lower slopes. I was told that Aconcagua is an extinct volcano. The ash we struggled over probably came from active volcanoes nearby.

Tupungato, about 50 miles to the south, has the highest volcanic cone I know of, at 22,310 feet above sea level. Farther north, from an airplane above the Tropic of Capricorn, I once saw scores of volcanoes higher than any in North America, but with little snow fringing their craters. This dearth of snow extends all the way from southern Peru to central Chile. Near the summits of about 30 such glacier-free mountains in the southern Andes stand ruins of shrines built by Inca worshipers at elevations up to 22,057 feet. From the peaks, half a dozen frozen cadavers of young male Indians have so far been recovered. Sacrificed to the sun by Inca priests in the 1470s, they had been killed by the cold.

One cone-shaped Andean peak in southern Bolivia, Cerro Potosí, holds the record for being the richest mountain on the continent, if not in the whole world. During the centuries after silver was discovered near its 15,827-foot summit in 1545, Cerro Potosí gained notoriety because of the countless Indian miners who slaved and died within its chambers. Driven by overseers' whips, they bored some 5,000 tunnels into the high-grade silver ore that veined the upper slopes, and they lived for days at a time in the bowels of the mountain. The city at its foot was one of the highest ever populated by Europeans; it is miserably cold, and barren despite heavy rain early in the year. Yet by 1660 it had become the largest and richest city in the New World.

After yielding silver that would be worth billions of dollars today, Potosí's lodes played out, and by 1825 the city's population had fallen from 150,000 to 8,000. But in the 20th century the place revived with the discovery that the heart of the mountain was veined with tin.

Now that heart is pierced by a deep vertical shaft from which tunnels branch outward. With its core deeply riddled, the mountain is almost all hollowed out. New diggings tend to collapse into long-forgotten galleries. The outer slopes are strewn with tailings piled upon tailings. Indian women sift through them ceaselessly, stuffing bits of tin ore into little handwoven woolen bags.

Many citizens of Potosí are trilingual. They speak Spanish, Quechua—the language of the Inca Empire—and Aymara, the tongue of pre-Columbian peoples who farmed the shores of Titicaca, the great lake 300 miles northwest of Potosí. During colonial times, Spaniards brought thousands of Indians from the Titicaca region to work in the mines.

I explored almost every cove and island of Lake Titicaca in my homemade cabin cruiser during the five and a half years I lived in Bolivia. Some inlets and shoreside villages were denied me by Indians who resented my approaching their fishing grounds. They were zealously defending newly won benefits of revolutions that had restored their ancient rights of ownership. It took no more than a single hail of bullets splashing close by to convince me that I was trespassing.

At 12,500 feet, Titicaca is the highest lake in the world navigable by large passenger steamers. Covering 3,200 square miles, it is so big that on a long cruise the mountainous shoreline astern falls beneath the horizon. Winter gales have such a long fetch and churn up such heavy seas that I often had to seek anchorage among dense reeds fringing the shore.

Indians use the reeds to build their graceful boats, to feed their cattle, and to build islands on which they construct dwellings of reeds. They use reed mats for walls, doors, roofs, and beds, and for drying fish. Reed stems fuel their earthenware stoves.

For me the main attraction of Lake Titicaca is the Island of the Sun, legendary birthplace of the Incas. The island's sprawling crags rise out of the lake like the spine and limbs of a gargantuan sea monster frozen by some magic spell. The labyrinthine stone palaces of Inca kings have fallen into ruin, but I once saw an unblemished white llama sacrificed to ensure a good harvest just as in the days of the lost empire.

Panpipe players and drummers led a serpentine line of dancers from the lakeshore to the summit of the Island of the Sun. On a windy hilltop a sorcerer slit the llama's throat at sundown and caught blood to sprinkle on Pacha Mama, Earth Mother. A kneeling woman held high a tray of burning incense, and a chill breeze wafted the fragrant smoke toward the far Peruvian shore of the sacred lake.

Another lofty lake in the central Peruvian highlands, Junín, at about 13,000 feet, won fame in a later period of Peruvian history. The plain surrounding the lake became the battlefield of Junín, where Simón Bolívar won his penultimate victory in the long struggle to throw off Spanish colonial rule. Before the end of this century, Junín may become better known as the farthest source of the Amazon.

Currently, the recognized source is a little lake named after me in the Mismi Massif of southern Peru. In 1971 I led an expedition to one of the summits, where meltwaters form the headwater brooks of the Apurimac. This river is the most distant tributary of the Amazon, according to detailed studies by the Peruvian Government, the Inter American Geodetic Survey, and National Geographic cartographers who measured the longest branch.

Since then, a consortium of six nations has begun to drill tunnels through the Andes to divert to the arid western slopes some of the Amazon headwaters that rage down the rain-soaked eastern side. When diversion tunnels eventually tap the upper Apurimac, meltwater from Laguna McIntyre will trickle down to new farmlands near the Pacific coast. Then the Amazon's most distant tributary will become Peru's Mantaro—the river that drains Junín.

Above the western edge of Junín rises the Continental Divide—a watershed only a hundred miles from the Pacific Ocean but two thousand miles from the Atlantic. Near the lake, the crest of the divide is marked by an array of pinnacles called the Bosque de Piedras—the Forest of Rocks. Countless towers of black stone blocks balanced precariously on top of one another stand as tall as California redwoods.

I used this impressive setting for an adventure film I helped produce in 1952. Since my citified crew could not carry on heavy work in the thin air, I hired Indians who lived in nearby stone huts that blended with the landscape of fluted spires.

When those Indians' ancestors first came here at least 12,000 years ago—near the end of the last great ice age—this part of the Continental Divide was a plateau of ancient volcanic rock still covered by ice, bits of which remain as small glaciers on nearby peaks. When the ice thawed, sometime before the Christian era, the underlying rock was exposed to weathering. Water seeped into the cracks, and alternating freezes and thaws split the rock. Today the forces of weathering continue their work in this black forest of sculptured stone.

Like the Bosque de Piedras, most of the natural wonders of South

"sprawling crags rise out of the lake like the spine and limbs of a gargantuan sea monster"

America fall into the category of "a great place to visit, but I wouldn't want to live there." Not so the volcanic highlands of Ecuador. So strong is their attraction for me that someday, when my wanderlust weakens, I shall surely be drawn to spend much of the rest of my life within sight of equatorial snow peaks.

From Quito, capital of Ecuador, you can see a glacier that flows from the Northern to the Southern Hemisphere. Its fissured ice inches down the southern slope of Cayambe, a dormant volcano that lifts its snow-clad summit just north of the Equator. The line crosses the glacier at 16,000 feet, the only place on earth where latitude and temperature both reach zero.

Several times I have attempted to follow the equatorial line from one side of the glacier to the other. But a deceptively smooth field of snow at the highest point hides a series of deep crevasses. Even with fine equipment and the best of climbing companions, I always turned back for fear of a sudden and perhaps fatal plunge.

A climber standing on top of Cayambe could hold his camera at exactly 19,000 feet above sea level and take a picture of the Amazon jungle to the east. On a clear day he might also photograph 16 solitary snow peaks, all but two of them volcanic in origin. Possibly his film would record a column of black smoke pouring from Sangay, the southernmost and most symmetrical cone—although it is blanketed nearly all the time with clouds that ascend from the Amazon basin.

On two occasions I have flown round and round Sangay's crater and watched it erupt, as it has throughout recorded time. Great blobs of lava whistle hundreds of feet into the sky and arch back down to pockmark the glistening snowfields of the upper slopes. The incandescent bombs have killed foolhardy climbers. Rivers of lava sizzle down through the most recent snowfalls. Although Sangay has been listed at 17,159 feet for more than 20 years, I would wager that, with so much activity, its elevation has changed.

Far more violent was the history of the next snow-covered volcano north of Sangay, known now as El Altar. The Incas called it Capac Urcu—Almighty Mountain. Indian legend tells that it exploded sometime before the Spaniards came, killing everyone for miles around and blackening the sky for years. Judging from the remnants of El Altar, the blast must have been far more powerful than the one that recently blew the top off of Mount St. Helens in Washington State. El Altar's caldera measures more than two miles across. Except for a gap to the west, the enormous pit is surrounded by a jagged arc of snowcapped pinnacles, some higher than Sangay. El Altar may have stood well above 20,000 feet before losing several cubic miles of ejecta in the blast.

In northern Ecuador, layers of ash from geologically recent eruptions are hundreds, even thousands of feet thick. Where builders of the Pan American Highway have cut deeply into mountainsides, you can count layer upon layer of ash: an 8-foot layer of brown capped by a 2-inch layer of white, then 11 inches of yellow and 12 feet of black, then another dusting of white, and so on.

At 20,561 feet, Chimborazo is the greatest of the Ecuadorian volcanoes. For centuries it was thought to be the highest mountain in the world, until exploration of Himalayan peaks in the early 1800s proved them to be higher. Measured from the center of the earth, Chimborazo

"Countless towers of black stone blocks"

is still the loftiest lump on the globe: The equatorial swelling of our oblate spheroid raises Chimborazo two miles higher than Mount Everest—though not when measured from sea level, the accepted procedure.

The volcano I like best is Cotopaxi, whose magnificent cone rises 35 miles south of Quito and can be seen from almost anywhere in town. Heat and steam keep its 2,000-foot-wide crater fairly free of snow, although its slopes are thickly glaciered. Cotopaxi's last major eruption was in 1877, when incandescent lava and gas melted its glaciers and sent disastrous floods down both its Atlantic and Pacific watersheds.

In 1966 two friends and I challenged Cotopaxi. We roped up massive glaciers that cracked and groaned with their ceaseless slippage down the steep slopes of lava and ash. When storms blanket the mountain with fluffy snow—neck-deep and avalanche-prone—not even expert mountaineers can climb Cotopaxi. But we had luck and reached the summit in nine arduous hours.

It was the tenth of August, Ecuador's Independence Day, and I felt wonderfully free up there above half the world's atmosphere. I stood at 19,347 feet, higher than I had ever climbed before. I could see almost all the way across that small nation, from the Amazon jungle to the Pacific Ocean. No daydream of my boyhood could match that spectacle of scattered white volcanoes towering above the green valleys of Ecuador—on a continent that holds so many natural wonders. I felt that I would be drawn back to this mountain time and again in years to come.

And I have been, every year or two. My latest visit was on May 16, 1982. Early that morning, just as I was making a photographic flight around Cotopaxi's crater, I saw a string of climbers gain the summit. They must have climbed all night and probably were not impressed by my reaching that great height the easy way. I took their picture.

I never learned who they were. But one of them may find the picture here, commemorating their conquest of my favorite mountain.

Bosque de Piedras—Forest of Rocks—bristles in the Peruvian Andes. This pinnacled landscape bears witness to centuries of weathering, as water and ice sculptured volcanic rock into giant pillars of stone up to 300 feet tall.

Overleaf: Dark specks in a realm of white, climbers reach the 19,347-foot summit of Cotopaxi, a snowcapped volcano only 50 miles south of the Equator in the Andes of Ecuador. Among earth's most active volcanoes, the peak claims its place in the profusion of nature's wonders.

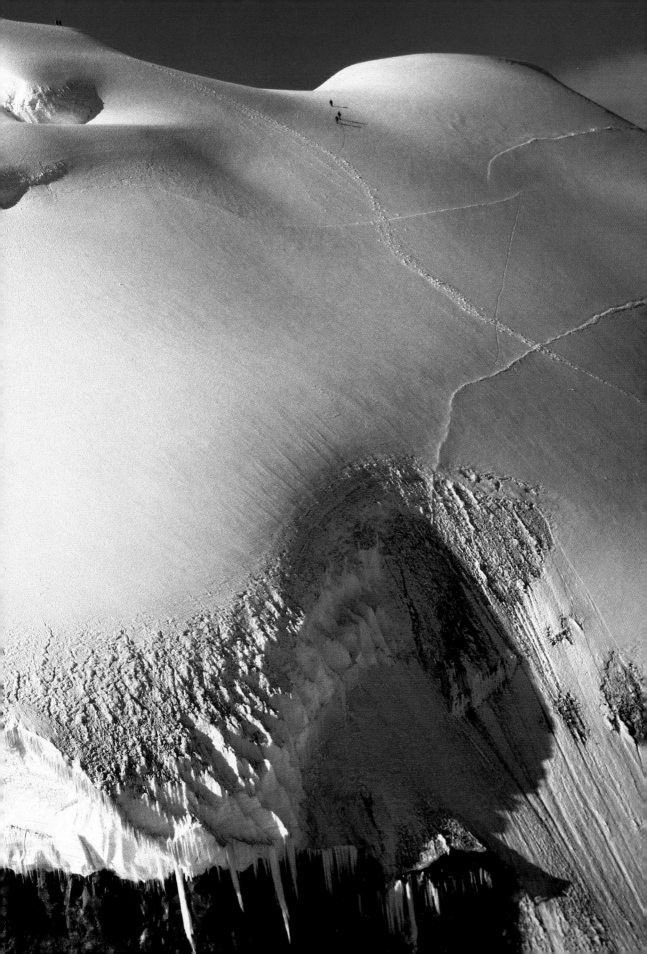

Notes on Contributors

Photographer DAVID AUSTEN, a native of Indiana, has spent virtually all his working life outside the United States, first in France, then in Australia and the Orient. Now based in Sydney, he has traveled on magazine and book assignments to nearly every Asian country and throughout much of the Pacific. He covered Papua New Guinea for a NATIONAL GEOGRAPHIC article in 1982, and has taken photographs for other GEOGRAPHIC stories.

PAUL CHESLEY has covered Death Valley, the Sawtooth Range, and the Continental Divide for Special Publications. His photographs have also appeared regularly in NATIONAL GEOGRAPHIC and other magazines, including *Geo*, *Smithsonian*, and *Fortune*. He has recently completed an assignment in the Southwest for the 1983 Special Publication *America's Hidden Corners: Places Off the Beaten Path*. Born in Red Wing, Minnesota, he now lives in Aspen, Colorado.

RON FISHER, a graduate of the Writer's Workshop at the University of Iowa, joined the Special Publications staff in 1966. He has written two Special Publications—*The Appalachian Trail* and *Still Waters, White Waters*—and has contributed chapters to several others. He is also the author of three Books for Young Explorers.

GEORG GERSTER, one of the world's foremost aerial photographers, lives in Zumikon-Zurich in his native Switzerland. He is the author-photographer of 15 books, among them *Grand Design*, *Brot und Salz—Bread and Salt*, and *Churches in Rock*. His work has been featured in *Geo* magazine, the London *Sunday Times Magazine*, NATIONAL GEOGRAPHIC, and several of the Society's books, including *The Desert Realm*.

WILLIAM R. GRAY journeyed around the world tracing the adventures of one of history's greatest explorers for *Voyages to Paradise: Exploring in the Wake of Captain Cook*. He backpacked the length of the nation for *The Pacific Crest Trail*, and he has traveled from Iceland to Tasmania, from Yugoslavia to Tahiti, for other National Geographic books. On the Society's staff since 1968, he is now an assistant director of Special Publications.

Now a resident of Virginia, LOREN MCINTYRE has lived in South America off and on for more than 35 years. Since 1966 he has written and taken photographs for nine NATIONAL GEOGRAPHIC articles on South American places and peoples. He is the author and photographer of a book on German naturalist Alexander von Humboldt and of a Special Publication, *The Incredible Incas and Their Timeless Land*. His work also appears in *The Desert Realm*; *Lost Empires, Living Tribes*; and other Society publications.

A NATIONAL GEOGRAPHIC photographer since 1961, California-born GEORGE F. MOBLEY has traveled the world on assignments ranging from the Amazon rain forest to reindeer herders in Lapland, from riots in Santiago to nomads in Rajasthan. He was the photographer for *The Great Southwest* and two Special Publications on Alaska, and has contributed to many other Geographic books. His extensive experience in the Arctic includes work in Greenland and Canada as well as Alaska.

A native of Champaign, Illinois, THOMAS O'NEILL has traversed much of North America since joining the National Geographic staff in 1976. He has written about Western explorer John Charles Frémont, the canyons of the Southwest, and the Canadian wilderness for Special Publications, and is the author of *Back Roads America: A Portfolio of Her People*.

New Yorker CYNTHIA RUSS RAMSAY lived in India and Iran before becoming a member of the Special Publications staff in 1966. She has covered subjects as varied as the Austrian Alps and small-town America, the Pacific Northwest and the ancient Mycenaeans. Writing assignments for *Splendors of the Past* took her to archaeological sites in Sudan and Sri Lanka.

N.G.S. PHOTOGRAPHER DAVID ALAN HARVEY

Richly tinted rock formations of Bryce Canyon National Park in Utah reveal nature's artistry. Millennia of weathering produced this haunting domain of cracked columns, delicate spires, and colossal stone fortresses. Nature ceaselessly shapes these and other wonders.

Composition for *Nature's World of Wonders* by National Geographic's Photographic Services, Carl M. Shrader, Director, Lawrence F. Ludwig, Assistant Director. Printed and bound by Holladay-Tyler Printing Corp., Rockville, Md. Color separations by the Lanman Progressive Co., Washington, D. C.; Lincoln Graphics, Inc., Cherry Hill, N.J.; NEC, Inc., Nashville, Tenn.

Library of Congress CIP Data:

Main entry under title:

Nature's world of wonders.

  Bibliography: p.
  Includes index.
  1. Physical geography. 2. Natural monuments. I. National Geographic Society (U. S.). Special Publications Division.
GB60.N27 1983   910'.02   82-47842
ISBN 0-87044-439-5
ISBN 0-87044-444-1 (lib. bdg.)

Index

Boldface indicates illustrations;
italic refers to picture captions.

Acknowledgments

The Special Publications Division is grateful to the individuals, organizations, and agencies portrayed, named, or quoted in this book, and to those cited here, for their assistance in its preparation: African Wildlife Foundation, David G. Ainley, Joan Anzelmo, Brian Baker, George Baker, Frederick M. Bayer, Charles R. Bentley, David Biederman, Sarah Bishop, Helgi Björnsson, William J. Breed, British Antarctic Survey, Shuhua Chang, E. H. Colbert, Ian Dalziel, Basil Davidson, David Deal, Harold E. Dregne, Robert H. Eather, Nils J. Ellström, Embassy of the Arab Republic of Egypt, Embassy of the Republic of Burundi, Embassy of the Republic of Kenya, Embassy of the United Republic of Tanzania, Geir Gjærde, Janet R. Gomon, Richard A. Gould, P. M. Green, Leif Grinde, Guy Guthridge, Chuck Hardy, Grant Heiken, Martin Heine, Robert Hole, Richard H. Howarth, Charles B. Hunt, Herschel Hurst, W. Timothy Hushen, Lute Jerstad, Mohammed Deen Khan, Kyozo Kikkawa, Hiroshi Kosumi, Karl Kranz, Philip R. Kyle, Philip E. LaMoreaux, Peter Lemieux, Joe McGowan, Magadi Soda Company, James Malcolm, Nanno Marinatos-Hägg, Marine Mammal Commission, Richard W. Marks, National Science Foundation (Division of Polar Programs), William Odum, Friedrich Oedl, Virgil J. Olson, John Palmer, Shea Penland, Bernard Prud'homme, R. Garry Rice, Dick and Jan Scar, D. J. Scarratt, Werner Schwerdtfeger, Haraldur Sigurdsson, Smithsonian Institution, Peter B. Stifel, Pat Tolle, Philip A. True, John R. Twiss, Jr., U. S. Botanical Gardens, U. S. Department of State, Deepak Vohra, David John Wakelin, Ron Warfield, John Waterbury, Florian Wetten, James Whittaker, Arnold G. Wilbur, John Younger, William J. Zinsmeister.

Additional Reading

The reader may wish to consult the *National Geographic Index* for pertinent articles, and to refer to the following:

GENERAL: Robert Decker and Barbara Decker, *Volcanoes*; Anthony Huxley, ed., *Standard Encyclopedia of the World's Mountains*; Walter Sullivan, *Continents in Motion: The New Earth Debate*. AFRICA: Leslie Brown, *East African Mountains and Lakes*; Sir Richard F. Burton, *The Lake Regions of Central Africa*; Elspeth Huxley, *The Challenge of Africa*; David Livingstone, *Missionary Travels and Researches in South Africa*; Alan Moorehead, *The Blue Nile* and *The White Nile*; Henry M. Stanley, *Through the Dark Continent*. EUROPE: Hjálmar R. Bárdarson, *Ice and Fire*; Ronald W. Clark, *The Alps*; Claire Eliane Engel, ed., *Mont Blanc*; J. V. Luce, *The End of Atlantis*; Julia E. Mullin, *The Causeway Coast*; Gaston Rébuffat, *Men and the Matterhorn*; Per Vogt, ed., *Norway Today*. ASIA: J. F. Bishop, *The Yangtze Valley and Beyond*; Edmund Hillary, *From the Ocean to the Sky*; J. S. Lall, ed., *The Himalaya: Aspects of Change*; George B. Schaller, *Stones of Silence: Journeys in the Himalaya*. AUSTRALIA AND THE PACIFIC ISLANDS: Isobel Bennett, *The Great Barrier Reef*; Erwin Christian and Raymond Bagnis, *Bora Bora*; Derek Roff, *Ayers Rock & The Olgas*. ANTARCTICA: Ian Cameron, *Antarctica: The Last Continent*; Jacques-Yves Cousteau, *The Ocean World of Jacques Cousteau: The White Caps*; U. S. Central Intelligence Agency, *Polar Regions Atlas*. NORTH AMERICA: Roger W. Brucker and Richard A. Watson, *The Longest Cave*; Hiram Martin Chittenden, *The Yellowstone National Park*; Marjory S. Douglas, *The Everglades: River of Grass*; Clarence E. Dutton, *Tertiary History of the Grand Cañon District*; Charles B. Hunt, *Death Valley: Geology, Ecology, Archaeology*. SOUTH AMERICA: Arthur Eichler, *Ecuador: Snow Peaks and Jungles*; John Hemming, *The Search for El Dorado*; Paul W. Richards, *The Tropical Rain Forest*; Helen and Frank Schreider, *Exploring the Amazon*.